Whispering Winds

Barbara Mary Bonner-Morgan

AuthorHouse™ UK Ltd.
500 Avebury Boulevard
Central Milton Keynes, MK9 2BE
www.authorhouse.co.uk
Phone: 08001974150

© 2009 Barbara Mary Bonner-Morgan. All rights reserved.

No part of this book may be reproduced, stored in a retrieval system, or transmitted by any means without the written permission of the author.

First published by AuthorHouse 11/17/2009

ISBN: 978-1-4490-1885-6 (sc)

This book is printed on acid-free paper.

To dear Diana & Geoffrey,
with love
from Rob & B B-M.

This book is dedicated to my dearly beloved husband Robin Peter Bonner-Morgan, our darling daughters and their spouses Sarah & Ian, Charlotte & James, Rebecca & Simon and Emma and their loving children Alexander, Luke, Saskia, William and Jabez

Contents

Golden Thread Of Love	1
St Peter Port - Arthritis	2
St Padarn Walked Here	4
The Welsh Mountains	5
Middle Aged Misery	6
Bourganvillia	8
The B-M Family	11
Save St Bartholomews Hospital London	15
St Bartholomews Hospital (Barts) Was Saved In February 1998	18
Holly And Jessica	20
Geoffrey	21
Emma's Vision Of Jesus Christ	23
The Family	24
Queen Elizabeth Jubilee Song	25
Mamma I Should Have Listened	28
A Century Of Sunbeam	29
Bring Back Ballroom Dancing	32
Mothers Stop Them Destroying Our World	33
William	37
JaBez	39
Primadonna Anna	40
Bernard Grahame	43
Sweet Jamie	50
One Man's Delight Is Another Man's Curse	53
A Guernsey Youth Orchestra	54
Spring In Lampeter	59
Learn To Be a Man Of God	61

Children Of Beslam	62
Ladder Of Love	63
Promiscuity Unhimges Civilisation	64
Yellow Fields	65
Mother Christmas	66
Snow Sprinkled Mountains	67
Enigma	68
Pure Soul	69
Tide's Right For A Sail In Guernsey.	70
Two Little Innocents Christmas Shopping At Boots In St Peter Port	72
Nails And Hoofs!	75
The Seigneur's Sons Eventually Make The Queen's Visit To Sark	76
The Drain Train	80
Jack The Gentleman Farmer	81
Spring	85
Beech Grove	86
Picnic Spot	87
Historic Brickwall Farmhouse	88
Tummies And Spirits	93
The Chicken Sale	94
The Everlasting Curridge Cottage Rose In Memory Of Geoffrey And May Shaw	97
All Slog And Slum At Oxford University -Amid World Class Education	99
Down Wind From A Cigarette Stoneleigh Station	102
Darling Child Full Of Fun	103
Jazzy Joctor	104
Lambs On The Hillside	105
Women Cleaners At The Bank	106
Kindly Work With The Elderly At Plas Padarn Wales	107

Disaster At Alfroques	109
Clemmie Churchill! That Painting !	114
Good And Evil	116
The Lord's Prayer	117
The Berlin Wall	118
Lovely Smells 1972	120
The Admiral's Roomsouthwold	121
Autumn 1993	125
The Family 1994	126
Hard Money Man	128
Man Of Straw	129
Beautiful Country Wedding	130
Wide Smiles	131
A Tough Christmas Time Encounter Banish The Tough Paired Police Traffic Zealots- Bring Back Our Dear Old Mr Plod?	132
Our Adorable Pets	134
Our Pond	135
Yobs	136
A Child's SecUrity And Happiness Is Found In Simplicity, Not Riches	137
Majestic Mountains 1992	138
Foxgloves 1992	139
Weeping Willow And Springdip Your Branches Willow Graceful	140
April	141
Welsh Castles	142
A Tribute To Grandpa	144
Get Up And Shake Up	146
Faith	147
Providence 2003	148
Baby Blue Tits 2003	149

World Mothers Stop This Crazy Nuclear Bomb Race	150
Summer 1987 Wales	152
The Exquisite Rose - A Tender Heart	153
Wedding Song Dawn And Eric 2004	154
Bluebells	155
9/11 Savaging Of New York	156
God In The GardEn At Plas Padarn	158
Mother Christmas Gives Joy To The Lonely Elderly And Needy	159
Rambla Nova Tarragona	161
Maggie The Great	163
Sycamore Autumn Scene	166
A Surprize Mother Christmas Meal For Mrs Kay On Christmas Day 1990	167
Jubilee Project 25 Years Of Queen Elizabeth 2 Guernsey-1977	170
Betty's Fuel	171
Julius Our Wonderful Golden Retriever	173
Last Day Of Finals At Oxford	174
Mr Major 'S Major Disaster	176
My Wonderful Husband	177
Exquisite Sunset	178
Child Abuse	179
Mother Christmas	180
Ladies ResTore Your Morals	182
The Loving Sisters Alex And Mary	183
2005 Bicentenary Of Nelson's Death A Pen Sketch And Verse On Horatio Nelson	186
Allegro In The Making	206
Deborah Bartram	236
John Peel (Ravenscroft) November 2004	238

Just William It's Fun To Be A Child Of Five	240
Elizabeth-Sarah	245
Mary-Julia-Charlotte	247
Susan-Rebecca	250
Margaret-Olivia-Emma	252
Channel Island Siege	255
Gillian And Virginia English Ladies Suffolk's Genteel, Devoted, Loving Sisters	259
Drusilla Mcleod 1932-2007 The Intended Lady Of Dunvegan Castle	262
Alex The Brave (Organ Scholar With Cystic Fibrosis At Eton College)	266
Judi Dench (Williams)	270
Joan Mary Eileen Ingpen 1916-2007	272
Rev. Canon Ronald And Myrtle Hares (1908-2007)	273
A Carol	274
Gloria B-M Briar House Residential Home For Mental Patients	275
My Mother Margaret Gwendoline Sarah Barnard (Nee Read)	282
Little Ba	302
Is There A Recipe For Golden Marriages?	303
Golden Wedding Anniversary	304
My Dearest Darling Beloved 50 Golden Years Of Happiness	306
Golden Anniversary Day	309
Thankyou Sweet Family	311
Darling Darling Family	313
State Stealing Babies	314
Beautiful Wonderful England	316
Untapped Medical Research	318
The Shaws	319
The Barnards	321
The Bonner-Morgans	325

Jeeralang Bush Fires Victoria Australia	332
Bush Fires	334
Paradise -Saved	339
Another Paradise -Saved	340
Sweet Child Of Heaven	341
Sweet Dean	342
Sweet Dean	344
Beef For The Boys	345
The B-M Diet That Has Been Found To Help Get Rid Of Symptoms Due To Food Intolerances	347
Spring	349
Lovely LadY Of Light-Diana's Departure	350
Sweet Angel Mayfly	352
Jesus	353
Abigail To Mummie Tara	354

Golden Thread of Love

Have you a Love which makes you weep
Deep and sweet and wonderful
A love unsullied by base sex
So pure in form of only heart beset
Love of parents for their sweet infant pure
Love of God for his flock secure
Love of a horse a dog a cat
Of a deeply caring nature that
This love links the whole of earth's creatures
A divine thread of gold
Parental-love the greatest feature
Happiness is measured on this
Thread of Gold
How much love in your heart
How much golden thread unfold
It is to God the strongest link
It costs nothing
Only kindly golden think
Open your heart to warmly give
Where there is need
Then you truly have the Thread of Gold
In divine happiness to live.

BMB-M

ST PETER PORT - ARTHRITIS

Young, agile creature, stepping high,
Bending stretching to the sky.
Dancing, laughing, running, jumping,
Endless energy, health ever surging.

What a contrast do we see
Sadly crippled unhappily.
Poor little lady bent in a chair
Unable to walk or comb her hair.
Wracked with pain, future formidable,
Frightened, frail joints immovable.
Oppressive, depressive, cruelly unjust,
This ghastly disease the joints to rust.
Of the bright active dancer, cutting her flight,
Creeping stealthily from site to site
Siezing up joints, rending them tight.
Limbs wasting thin from diminished use,
Brave her spirit, courage profuse.

Kindly ladies arrange the flowers,
Clothe the Town Church throughout the hours.
Talented practised musicians chime,
Augment sacred stone with music fine.
The belfry's time-honoured hymn tunes are peeling,
Gulls in the harbour delighted are wheeling.
Shoppers crowding on the cobbled street,
Delay their purchases, and at the Church do meet.
Donating generously, spirits uplifted,

In this place of Grace befitted.
The organ fills with wondrous sound,
Choirs sing their message with new joy found.
Instrumentalists, beauteous harmony creating,
Wonderfully contributing, perfection making.
A united effort for others to see,
Thoughts directed to relieve misery.
For this caring, shared alliance,
Helps research in medical science
To isolate the joints offence
To alleviate the plague immense.
Let warmth and help be this gift of ours
In this sacred setting of music and flowers.

BMB-M

ST PADARN WALKED HERE

In ancient times a Monk walked here
St Padarn was his name
A cross he bore around his neck
And goodness was his fame
In prayer he graced this beauteous spot
And sick his help did seek
He gathered wood in summer-time
To warm the winter bleak
A simple life and vespers heard
Around the river plains
Others joined this goodly throng
St Padarn was his name
A simple wooden building
They erected on the slope
And placed a cross aloft
And raised that sign of hope
Many devils crossed his path
With strength he them dispatched
For where ever great the goodness lay
Evil seeks to equal match
Today his mission starts again
As St Padarn's clinic rise
His person mount upon the roof
As guard, cross raised to skies
Great goodness here will ever dwell
And evil fight and evil quell
The sick will rise their health restored
And they will praise their goodly lord. 13.11.90

BMB-M

THE WELSH MOUNTAINS

What mystery shimmers in the mountains
The shadows of excitement afar
Etching hither and thither from the mistland
Soft pale blue grey pastel peninsula
Far distant sea lapping as carpet
Cloudless sky soaring with birds on the wing
And here I stretch round to lambs on the hillside
Welsh primroses profuse shining light around ring
Violets almost forgotten, dandelions bold in their hue
Birds singing pairing and flirting
Three horses gallop fresh in the dew
Here life is so strong real and active
But those mountains enigma pervade
As my eyes cast to far undulations
Their wispy outlines excitement have made.

BMB-M

MIDDLE AGED MISERY

You're a middle age misery
Job mastery achieved
Monotonous routine
Unrelieved
You feel like a clerk
In the dreary array
Excellence must dismiss the fay
Delight in newness long gone by
Responsibility has heavy lie
Creativity one now must choose
In order boredom to completely lose
Where to follow this elusive ray
Where do we look to lighten our day
It lies where least suspected
In the farthest spot we could have elected
One must not look to distant places
To new vistas and new faces
As a cure for middle age moan
That way the syndrome returns too soon
The awful danger of too many riches
Is too many fields
And not enough ditches
Its knowing nature that gives us grace
And with grace comes smiling face
There for us all to enjoy
Away from ugly material cloy
Its in creativity we grow
We only reap where we do sow

And polishing up our personal relationship
That in our family we give more friendship
The moans will melt the sadness change
Delight and fun your life rearrange
Get out the paint pot
Study flowers and birds
Then the thought of misery becomes absurd
Your work take on a brighter hue
As your leisure and hobbies gives more to do
Sport will also relieve the spell
As exercise takes oxygen to the farthest cell

BMB-M

BOURGANVILLIA

Two little grandsons
Were on the rocks to fish
Basking in the Spanish sun
To fill their nets they wish
Grandpa watchful by the sea
As patiently they waited
Why would they so avoid their rods
So elaborately baited.
They sat and sat
And sighed and sighed
These poor sad lads no fish espied
So up the three and home did go
No fish for grannie's platters
But never mind
I'm sure she'll find
A few crumbs for the latters
Soon tums requite
They all did sight
A lengthy bourganvillia
So tempting there, so colourful
Just waiting on the sillia
'Twas near the balcony below
From whence its origins did grow
But none above did flourish now
But beauty back some 40 years
Our balcony too this flower then bears
It was a sight of wonder
But cruel shears did steal our flowers

And cut them down asunder
We now must fish this flower dish
Whilst length it did exhibit
And drag it forth
Our rail to sport
Before the shears inhibit
The boys with net and rod did fish
With energy to tame this dish
With push and pull and many a blip
They did not stop 'til caught their slip
Their proud and smiling grandparents there
Were thrilled with this persistent pair
For now that wondrous flower would thrive
Upon their balcony alive
So tied with string, triumphant strand
Would once more thrive
So close at hand
Tenderly they all observe
And wait the following year with verve
And hope the obvious climbing stand
Would be noticed by the gardeners hand
Ganny and Ganpa to Spain the following year
Hardly dared the balcony peer
Shattered they found the ugly shears
Had cut the darling strand, what tears
The delicate end dangled snatched
Its precious life sap cruelly snatched
There'd be no flowers this year to love
On our balcony up above
What would the boys say when they knew
That their efforts were appreciated by so few
But Ganny up and planted the end

As a cutting she would be its friend
Much water and love on it bestowed
Maybe still life in it did flow
So on the balcony in gathered soil
Ganny hopes reward will suffice her toil
Flowers abundant the following year
Will adorn with purple the balcony bear.
Come bourganvillia flourish now
With so much love on you bestow. 17.2.02

BMB-M

The B-M FAMILY

Cosy family open the door
And there we see the daughters four
Pretty, charming, fun & intelligent too
Horses and music the theme song through
Australia in 10 acres of bush run free
With Koala bear up yonder tree
Snakes and bushfires, roos and wallabies
Eucalyptus statuesque, golden sand and mountain seas
Pinny and Dinah gallop and frisk
In the paddock follow their carefree brisk
Daughters in the roughest school
Never mind they find it cool
Daddy and Mamma most priviledged care for eyes
With surgery or physician which ever requires
Cataracts, squints, retinal detachments and corneal grafts
Blind to see and great joy given through surgical crafts
Jeeralang also cattle and tennis for fun
Later Sale expansion of huge practice begun
Grand old farmhouse with wisteria festooned
Round veranda and beauty honed
With groups of friends much fun extend
Off to Melbourne even Shakespeare lend
Pleasant flat in Toorak smart
But friends insist with them
The nights to start
Wonderful life and income high
But for home the hearts did sigh
Seven years before to Europe return

England and Suffolk keenly yearn
Guernsey first to catch the eye
An ophthalmic surgical practice on this Island spy
Bourg de Bas farmhouse near Petit Bot
Was an excellent spot for happiness to sow
Daffodil fields and acres free
Choir in Town Church and boats on the sea
Ancient Isle of friendship and charm
And relaxing calves donkey and fruit on the farm
Family would never see a happier time
Than on this friendly magical Island fine
Musically acclaimed Allegro game, tennis, sailing, friends galore
Reluctant leave this island paradise for children's future store
Father finds consultant eye surgeon post in family linked Wales
For parents to be closer if children experienced problems or frail
But immensely dreary devoid of lively social fun we'd known
Except tall mountains, music and fine house Plas Padarn blown
Later much joy with frail elderly regenerate anew
Giving love and warmth to cheer their latter years so few
Our first daughter early music after Ozzie global tour
Wonderful experiences exciting cultures draw
Her dear friend would her wed
But she a career lady chose career instead
Striding the world with music of highest kind
Tourguide and organiser of concerts fine
Soon Oxford New College Wedding romance to fly
Our second beautiful daughter her perfect man, love's sigh
Mother, later doctor radiologist and two sons born
Whilst her husband achieves Aldenham headmaster dawn
These young boys choristers in London's St Pauls
Immense music excellence this position calls
And exquisite third finds a graduate of Oxford to wed

A second daughter up the aisle in Wales Llanbadarn led
A son and daughter they produce to their delight
Whilst husband deputy head in public school
Wife in T.V. and P.R. efficient smart and cool
Making films and of two a great Mum
A daughter first and then a son
At Daddy's school they grew and thrived
In Shenfield a busy smart well indulged life
Eyes still mainstay of parents occupation
No part time surgery for dual satisfaction
Mother Christmas scheme for lonely Christmas relieve
London Concert and some acclaim nationwide receive
But hearts relish back to East Anglia to Browston come
Later a divine Tudor farmhouse in Wetherden among
Fourth daughter songwriter to Oxford for Mandarin Chinese to learn
All four daughters and their children of Shaw genes in abundance turn
This one finds this Shaw music her primary interest take
As lone Mum of fine musical sporty son a hard life herself she make
Three Cathedral choristers two St Pauls and one Bury bred
With music sport and singing ever in their head
Alternating with rowing canoeing tennis and sailing
Wide interests much fun their lives now hailing
Firstborn at last finds her love in Edinburgh's northern reach
After graduate and great life in early music finest
Now healing Alexander teach
So four beautiful joyous daughters happy with their lot
Two great teacher son-in-laws and 5 fun grandchildren begot
B-M lives always enhanced by gold labs and retrievers
And of horse and pussie cat love the great givers and receivers

Artistic and country interests, theatre, books add to medical life
Spanish family holidays help all relax from daily grind and strife
Always time for God, prayers and church attend
Great kindness to this close little family He lend
Deep love and affection and now 50 golden years together
With God's help in warm embrace we'll stay like this for ever
Retirement's a new experience after an exhuberant lifetime
In peace and love with joyous family let life naturally recline
Content abundant happiness with family sweet achieve
We cherish 50 Golden years and hope celebrate more before we leave

BMB-M

SAVE ST BARTHOLOMEWS HOSPITAL LONDON

Founded in 1123 by Rahere

Shine brightly moon in sky mysterious starred
Shine bright on Barts, its future may be scarred
Uneasy in its bed
Decisions roll uncertain o'er its head
Helpless in torment racked
As its great will to heal the sick
Is sacked
Bravely born down centuries past
To other uses may be rudely cast
How comes this cruel crunch to bear
On Barts the brave which only wants to care.
Accursed bureaucrats, do you not see
That Barts should greatest place of healing be
To teach the young midst history of times gone
Did not its wall give comfort
To the plague ridden throng
Hush! As Rahere stoops, his furrowed brow
Anxious and sad, his bent form bow
Hasten to rescue Barts his blessed dream bestowed
As plain song rose a smile himself allowed.
Foundation here on hallowed ground
The choir crescendo loud their beauteous sound
Hospital and monastery strong in blessed link
Except for Barts the Great the monastery sink

Let not the scavengers of market forces
Bury Barts for monetary resources
We'll band and fight each stone to guard
Draw swords, we'll every ill intention bar
Fear not most noble Barts
Your children wield their forces now to start –
Boom the great bell of Barts the Great and Barts the less
Drive out the devil of our distress
Ring out the rescue, gather clans around
Think swiftly Barts to make secure abound.
Sink not in sad despair
We children of your walls
We fight and we are there
Shine softly moon through windows ancient tall
As beams fall on the famous Hogarth wall
Beam softly through the wards
Where doctors fight each life to save
When battle lost the nurses gently sooth the brave
Welcome new babes glimpsing life's first light
Barts born, cradled, christened womb flown flight
Hark moon shed light on fountain splash
Where ancient throngs of rugby lads cut boisterous dash
Lend your beams where plane trees shade the square
Til recent, when the storm laid bare
The shade where sweet love blossomed in times past
These loves are strong and bound to last
Cast beams upon the lists of sponsors glad
Upon the walls of ancient hall in beauty clad
Officials governmental touch not a single hair
Of our beloved Barts, or shake in fear
Drive off your savage blows or find our sword
For Rahere stood Barts here to please his Lord

This twelfth century jester turned miraculous monk
Guide us and guard this place
We'll see this devil sunk
Great Barts will stay for centuries more
To cure the sick its past and future store
Ring loud the bells of Barts the Great
And moon shine bright and guide the beams of fate 11.11.92

BMB-M

St BARTHOLOMEWS HOSPITAL (BARTS) WAS SAVED IN FEBRUARY 1998

And we did fight for 5 years until <u>Barts was saved</u>
My husband Robin and I set up the 'Doctors Save Barts'. We made a gigantis of Rahere the Augustinian founder of Barts (A.D.1123).

I wrote a news letter every Friday which were distributed round the libraries in London and faxed round all the media and to Canada and the U.S.A..
A website was set up.

We cqmpaigned every Sunday outside Henry V111th gate. Our team followed all leads ready to drive to hot spots at a moments notice with our huge banners and Rahere..

The Daily Mail published 4 of my letters. I spoke on the London radio dozens of times and also on national BBC T.V.

We dressed in operating gowns for major events and once held up P.M. Major for ½ hour from entering Parliament when vast numbers of students in operating gowns took the gigantis of Rahere the Augustinian monk who founded Barts Hospital in 1123A.D., on his wheels, and ran round Parliament Square, a wonderful and rare sight.

We took a large delegation to Brussels submitting a petition on the grounds of Human Rights

We were determined to win and it was said our impact was enormous. We started our campaign when everybody said it was a lost cause and nothing would save Barts. There had been a huge effort by the consultants and the patients campaign.

After Barts was saved we continued as 'The Watchdog for Barts' and went on the London Parade every new years day for 10 years taking the gigantis Rahere with our wonderful faithful team of supporters.

HOLLY AND JESSICA

God's Heavenly Light
Has shone on Soham
Where the evil one had been
A million flowers of love now
Where sweet girls had graced the scene
Love abundant shining
Round the ancient Church of God
Where these adorable girls
Attended Church from the cradle
Their tiny feet had trod
Now they view as angels
The love their lives had left
God's treasure's arms enfolding kin
So cruelly now bereft

1.9.02 BMB-M

GEOFFREY

His world was dark
Through blindness
Yet he was light
As in the morning dew on grass
Lit as if 'twas a thousand candles
By the sun of dawn
So clear his mind at 98
So disciplined we find
His heart of gold
A father adored
Of all within his fold
And yet none of his own
This Colonel and lawyer renown
Articulate amusing of strongly held views
Witty and once read the BBC news
Though Welsh a quintessential Englishman
Courteous kind immensely independent
And of crystal clear mind
Golf enthusiast
But with brilliant Blofeld commentary graphic
In his blindness became cricketing fanatic
His relatives visits lit his life
He dearly missed his dear wife
As he aged more the more special he became
Uncomplaining, darling blind helpless and lame
He unearthed great kindness
Invaluable to those he knew

His warmth to radiate and benefit
Far beyond his view
Our lives have lost a golden light
Of courage strength and fun
His journey into god's great love Undoubtedly just begun
At last his eyes will see again And find the light so bright
And see those precious faces missed Since blindness took his sight
12.12.05

BMB-M

EMMA'S VISION OF JESUS CHRIST

A vision pure I saw that day
Of Jesus Christ in golden glow
As Louis Pallau told of him
The remarkable tale of old
The vision tall in long pale robes
As looked I to the side
Did dominate the stairway
And still with me abide
The eyes were sweet and loving
Such beauty did me strike
So strong and clear and wonderful
I never saw the like
The hands in sign of blessing
That he bestowed on me
Then just as quickly did appear
More quickly did it flee
And in monastic garden peace
My heart with joy did pound
So strong my urge to sing and cry
With beauty all around
For there in Aberystwyth
I did see the Lord
And want to spread this message
To the millions who've not heard
By music spread this miracle
Of sweetness rarely seen
And spread the dearest blessing
That happiness may they glean.

9.5.94 BMB-M

THE FAMILY

The family is a pool of love and friendship
A healing balm to all within its bounds
Each giving and taking of its replenishment,
Each experiencing its ups and downs.
Its paths of approach may vary
And often thistles may be found
Especially prickling fair tender feet
If arrogance and selfishness are around.
Before best healing balm is taken
Selfishness must be forsaken.
From its hugs a warmth emerges
From its kisses sweetness flows
Immense benefits with club restrictions
Every member surely knows
If restrictions recognise
Prevents the cracks and compromise
With unquestioning love
Loves each loves all
Succouring temperature
Does not fall
To wallow in the shallows
Or swim in centre warm
Gives solace from the big hard world
And happiness finds dawn.
The perfect situation to give more than one gets
And in return gets infinite more
Than any one gives

20.5.94 BMB-M

QUEEN ELIZABETH JUBILEE SONG

Let's celebrate, let's celebrate
Our Queen of 50 years
Who brightens with her wondrous smile
As on her head
Our crown she bears
Light up our divine and lovely land
With the dazzle of your smile
With a mother, sunshine love
That only a mother can beguile
For Briton's mother amazing sure you are
With 50 years its servant, Queen and star
Silent crowned at a great height
High in Kenya, Africa, at dead of night,
As elephants, lions and zebras feed
And silhouettes of fleeing gazelles take heed
Enchanted, close, she with her loving prince
The two young lovers astonished stare
That she was Queen quite unaware
From their simple fig tree house
Gazing at the water hole
Both silent
Quiet as mouse

Queen Elizabeth the second
Our pride and love now beckon
Faultless duty dedication
Stirs our grateful admiration
50 years we now have seen

Of our much loved
Christian Queen supreme

Let's celebrate, let's celebrate
Our great Queen Elizabeth's Jubilee
And appreciate our lovely land
So fair and kind and free.

A burden heavy
On your slender shoulders drift
As sadly from your Kingly
Father's body spirit lift
Now gone this instant
Happy family carefree days
Poorly substituted
With hollow adulatory praise
Adorned with fine clothes
For which you care not E'en a jot
Curious eyes peering from every angle
Privacy scarce, a sorry lot
Every luxury but a family sore deprived
Of you their loving
Mother attentive by their side
A mother shared with Commonwealth
Your diplomacy respected
Far greater than any yet
President elected
Everybody's mother
Yet now could mother none
Your children's arms reach out
To reach their unreachable sun
Your Prince now double parental

Role must view now to embrace
As less of his beautiful wife
He and their children must surely face
Horses are your hobby
And many dogs your known delight
Family relaxations snatched from
The stresses of your might
Sandringham, Balmoral, Windsor
Wellies for country mud do keep
When not at Buckingham Palace
For great duties you both sleep.

BMB-M

MAMMA I SHOULD HAVE LISTENED

Mamma I should have listened
When you told me those things
To practice restraint then
Romance from that springs
Instant sex could make man
A cruel and mean commodity
Unwilling to commit
As in restraint and chastity
When another side of him emerges
Kind and soft and sweet respect
And infinite more commitment
To his chosen lady elect
So much more enchanting
Flirty fun on the wing
Now I shall listen
To your wise-to-marriage-thing.

BMB-M

A CENTURY OF SUNBEAM

One hundred years
Great hunks of English oak
This mighty smack is still afloat
Up the sails
And thro' the Heads
Of Lowestoft Harbour
Adventure treads
High the waves
And howls the gale
To Dogger Bank
With trawl and sail
Rolling and swaying
In storm and hail
On this great hulk of oak
Sailors mauled
By salt and soak
Hard this life
And cold the knarled hands
Ton weight clothing
But friendship bands
Harsh the spray
And winds most cutting
But triumph reigns
When shoals a sighting
Shouts as trawl is loosed and falls
To drag the deep and 'net-full' calls
Skipper shouts the trawl to hold
As fills the ship with protein gold

Slippery decks, but man soon righted
If not his loving family blighted
Silver shimmer fill the ship
Until its full, no more to tip
Slater and Barnard fleet abobbing
In storm
Their families pray, asobbing
Abob on the ocean
On the cruel North Sea
Danger to scorn
No where to flee
When calm and out at sea on Sunday
The smacks in a circle tied
And thanked their Lord for safe delivery
From stormy times, when might had died
They lusty sang their songs of praise
As gulls swooped and water lapped with laze
34 smacks their sails a blown
Jostling bobbing, ships aflown
All to fish the North Sea cold
For white fish, as the fishermen of old
These 80 feet giants
Brave crews aboard
To fill English tables
With cheap fish afford
Sailing in storm and adrift in dead calm
Families praying they'd return without harm
Sailing magnificence
Tall ships with red brown sails
Turmoil or still whether calm or gales
Until late 1930s a beautiful sight
Then sold to Sweden as engines made blight

Faster than sail to the fish grounds gold
No fish, no boats, no crews, so sold
John Barnard could not Slater persuade
When a buyers huge bid was made
Disappointed buyer an engined fleet built
The sailing fleet gradually out of kilt
Sad and obsolete no longer the best
Sold to Sweden for retirement and rest
Beauty and strength to the Fiords go
Lowestoft sadly stoops to progress now
There to sail the fiords wonder
Transporting passengers
Mid calm and thunder
Much treasured for their beauty and size
Safe dependable
Security there lies
Sunbeam back after 70 years
To celebrate its century of triumph and tears
Back to its place of birth
Lowestoft Suffolk
Where it first touched earth
Back with Tomas Hellstrom
Mad about the smack
Deodar's owner and skipper
To Lowestoft back
Side by side through the famous Heads
Stately, joint-sailing, magnificence weds
God Bless you God speed you
Intrepid smacks
'Til safely arrived in Stockholm back

BMB-M

BRING BACK BALLROOM DANCING

Where has all the dancing gone
That bound in sweet romance
Twirling steps around the floor
To music of the dance
Hand in hand and arms around
Eye to eye and sweetness bound
Steps all learned at school or other
Off to hops with friends and brother
Ladies dressed so sweet allure
Eyes to meet across the floor
Quickstep, polka dance and waltz
Time assess whether kind or false
Centuries bind the young romance
We must see magic in the dance
Rock and roll to sex explore
But traditional dance romance adore
Bring it back to marriage bind
And enchant all young in life's young find.

BMB-M

MOTHERS STOP THEM DESTROYING OUR WORLD

Earth mothers
From loving homes
Busy caring for families
As since time hath lent its loan.
Out with your screwdrivers
And dismantle evil arms
Intent on evil missions
At which our quaking earth now qualms

If not your pain at bearing
Your infant, at the breast,
Will all to no avail
For they'll be blasted
Scorching to their rest

Stand for Parliament
Sit not back and gaze
Too many past decisions
Were taken
Far beyond our ways.

Set up a mother Party
To protect that which we've born
Leave it not to the foolish
That'll have us of life shorn.

Earth mothers gather
From every land arise
Get out your brushes
And sweep these nuclear evils
From our skies.

Dismantle the dinosaurs
Use the bits to build abodes
And benefit the homeless
And the poor with little food.

Creation was placed
Trusting in our wombs,
And we've allowed destroyers
To set the fatal doom
For we mothers hold within our hands
Creation, equalled never.
Arise and beat the politics
Before this life they sever.

The baby in its cradle
The family warm and snug
The cosy home protected
Within cosy parent rug.
The books that fill the library
The art upon the wall
Music and medicine
In suicide will fall.
Loving domestic animals
Gazelles within the park
Tall aging oaks a-stretching
All will lose their heart.

Wondrous buildings lovely landscape
Birds delirious on the wing
Blooming flowers in summer
Joyous children's voices ring.
Computers in their brilliance
Man probing into space
All be lost forever
In this lunacy of hate.
The ugly nuclear devils
They'll not decide our fate
This race must stop immediately
Before it's far too late.
Out with your screwdrivers
Dismantle evil arms
Intent on evil missions
Before which our quaking earth now qualms.
Great Ladies of Greenham
St Joans of modern day
We mothers give you full support
To drive these arms away.
Our babes must be protected
From the mushrooms East and West
And since the powers have failed us
We must take up this quest.

Mothers unite
From every land arise
Join hands and rid our lovely earth
Of suicides demise.
St Joans for-gather
Be strong in your resolve
Lest lovely life hereafter

Is rent of its revolve.
Mothers be the watchdog
Watch carefully those that play
Tin soldiers
Turning nuclear
To blast our World to fray.

BMB-M

WILLIAM

William is a frogging master
Froggies ever hopping faster
Newts and toads and frogs all slimy
Slip and slop in hands so tiny
Seeking under every stone
Slimy creatures find their home
Bosom pals spend hours of play
In the watery bucket day
Shrieks of tinies "found another"
Before poor creature jumps for cover
Hours of blissful nature play
Jabez and William spend their day
Tabby puss curls in a ball
Blackie puss tight ropes on the wall
Marti neighs excited loud clear
Longing to trot in the hay field freer
He's great at footie, swimming too
Violin and piano practice must do
Tennis ball gets hardest wack
Watch out I'll get it back
And wow his reading is so quick
But numbers need clearing
And seem to be up to tricks
At school he's got a lot of friends
Play hide and seek make secret dens
Beavers is fun with a nature ring
Then they sit and have a sing
Spanish kids are special fun

He's known them since was only one
Choir singing in Bury Cathedral grand
Is the greatest honour, Mr Thomas command
He adores his 4 cousins but specially Jabbie
Of all his animals its little Tabbie
And don't forget Ganny Ganpa and his Mummie
For do they not find yums for tummie

BMBM

JABEZ

Jabbie loves his dinosaurs
Horses, wows and pussies paws
Froggies leaping in the leaves
Toadies hiding in the caves
He knows an eagle and many birds
And can spell some three letter words
,At reading books he is so clever
But eating sausages he says no! never!
He loves tennis, rugby and football too
And could kick goals the whole day through
Magnetic games are really fun
He adores his toys just everyone
William is his best friend ever
Together fun their best endeavour
Swimming frogging pussy play
They're happy together all the day
Shouting laughing kicking balls
Only tears if unfortunate falls
They run and jump and swing and dive
And are only William six and Jabez five
Special too Sassie Daddy and Mummie
For do they not find yums for hungry tummie

BMB-M

PRIMADONNA ANNA

Anna is a prima donna
She just screams for what she wanna
Til she stops chaos does reign
This silly child
Is a right, real pain
She'd have us grovelling at her feet
This behavioural trend we must unseat
Poor Mum is in a frightful dither
This pickle makes her all aquiver
She vows to never brush her hair
Wow! What a fright! What a scare!
Face, so pretty, sticky red with jam
But she won't wash it, tho' she can
What neglect of a beautiful face
We would call it a right disgrace
She'll wear purple, but shrieks at pink
Hates dresses, but will wear trews, she fink!
Won't sit nicely at the table
But fidgets and jitters as much as she's able
Manners appalling, tools in the air
Food flung over the table in Jabez's hair
Her parents sigh in deep despair
They really must apply for a new au pair.
Her bedroom so tidy at the start
She flings clothes all around
It breaks one's heart
When she climbs in bed at night
To rest this awful, naughty fright

She reads trendy Auril the Skater cool
But won't read books sent home from school
This intelligent child is a right real shocker
She must surely straighten up her rocker
Will we need an oligist
To fathom out this pickle fish?
No most certainly not we'll not that need
For it seems misunderstanding
This behaviour feed
Momentous truths give notice why
This naughty child is all awry
Unwitting teacher at her school
Is responsible for Anna playing the fool
This teacher said one day at school
When class was quiet and cool
"I do not care how you behave at home
But when you're here this is how it's done"
So home to wreck they all resolve
For wasn't that what teacher told
Anna took this very serious
And home to wreck the place delirious
Whilst at school an 'angel' is
Still and quiet and tidy bliss
As were all the others too
But shocking at home, the Mums were through
The Mums had had enough, were wild!
All were complaining about each naughty child
So en mass they march up to the school
Shoulder to shoulder and not at all cool
Intent to see teacher and commanding tell
Their children are being taught
To create a living hell

Poor teacher, quakes as Mums gain pace
For retribution raw is in their face
"But mothers dear, I've not you forsaken
I'd never offend, something's mistaken
At home, obedient too, I would
My sweet little doves I find so good
And Anna find the best of all
Her star ladder is both laden and tall
They could and should and must and will
Go home and clean the wreck they spill
No more behaviour unseemly and bad
That's all in the past for these children so mad
Of course I care how at home they conduct
Clean, tidy and biddable my adorable ducks
From now on a great improvement you'll see
Now, just you calm down Mummies
Go off for a nice cup of tea."
Now smiles from scowls came at the double
As they envisaged order from home chaos and muddle.

BMB-M

BERNARD GRAHAME

Suffolk
Grahame he was a bonny child
Round and fair and blue
A lusty cry from Holly farm
Was the first his family knew
Born to farm, a farmer's son
In country and land he'd find his fun
Feet in wellies, trod the mud
In Barnby, 5th of 6 young Suffolk buds
Then came Hitler's war to shake
Each in his bed to shudder make
Planes flew thick across the shore
Bombs crush Lowestoft by the score
So Jack took his family to safer land
Tenanting Holly Farm to hand
Rumburgh by Halesworth now their home
White House Farm here they were come.
Sheltered on their Grandpa's estate
Away from Hitler's vicious aerial hits of hate
Yummy Sunday meals at Wissett Lodge Manor —house scene
Never better, though, than Mummie's cuisine
Seated formally around Monks medieval table long
Supported by carvings of the twelve Apostles strong
Exquisite carved oak chairs with tapestry fine padded
Matching ancient blues of ancient tapestries
Over extensive oak panelled walls added
Crisp white table linen and solid silver service gleaming
Five grandchildren's manners and speech

Underwent scrutinous screening
'What happened to those Ts Bar and sit up straight
Between mouthfuls place your knife and fork nicely on your plate
Never speak when eating and wait to be spoken to first
Take polite sips and not a drop of spillage to quench your thirst'
Jack Barnard family at another Barnard -White House
Rumburgh farm
Jack and Margaret to work with war depleted servant alarm
Fighting heavy land, devoid of a dozen farmhands and cold
Medieval mod cons in their farmhouse old
But this family grew strong and fine
With lusty voices in tune and time
Margarets lovely voice singing through all trouble and toil
As she strove to keep immaculate cleanliness amid huge house soil
Keeping family fed and warm in freezing winters chill
Images of tinies in nighties candlelight eager faces fill
No running water but that pumped water from the cobbled
courtyard stands
Now but one village Mrs Killick cycles to help where pre-war
several hands
Barely a labourer to help poor struggling Jack upon the farm
Would arouse in his wife and family much concern and alarm
The heroism of battling farmers was as great as frontline force
Trying to feed the army, to fight Hitler, with no help or resource.

But children blissfully unaware
Of the wartime strife to maintain their care
Mid, 4 seasons of colour change on land
A joyful life with nature close at hand
Swinging in the willows as leaves in water dipped
Young Grahame slipped in the drink, his life nearly pipped
But big sisters close at hand,

Hauled him out to drier land
To towels and anxious parents dear
Their little squibs had little fear
But saved he was and meant to thrive
To celebrate his sixty five
And courage he needed for black clouds gather nigh
As his devoted Daddy was taken to his maker on high
After slaving for his youngsters for 13 years
Through their laughter fun and tears
Now the role of angel care
O'er each child his guidance bear
This sudden calamity with broken hearts
Next night Wisset lodge near broke apart
A Lancaster bomber missed by a whisker mere
Crashing to smash all windows near
Their sanctuary at once destroyed
Each child to a separate home deployed
It was but Christmas in 5 days time
Those kindly Barnards put on a party fine
Before the family of kiddies five
Were sent hither and thither to grow and survive
As Christmas Bells rang in 1943
They'd not for 4 years a close family be
Adoring mother, distraught, expecting her sixth
Savage the blows which she was betwixt
A loving mother and wife was she
No better would you ever see
Widowed and now her children to lose
Shattered, cruel life, confuse
Grahame to his father's sister did go
And a nice cousin continued life's flow
Another blow his family take

Grandpa in twelve months this life forsake
Father and Grandfather but a year between
Seldom was such sadness seen
But this tot was young and times pass
And the life of the moment is all they ask
Happy on the farm, his wellies in the mud
As he sat on the tractor and saw cows chew the cud
Once more a farmer's lad miniscule
In no time at all he was off to school
He grew a strong and caring lad
On the farm with Joe as his dad
His real family grew apart
Wrenched from its loving dearest heart
His life progressed along just fine
Until he was just nearly nine
His mother pined to have her six
It broke her heart to have space betwixt
Ne'r mind smart school the Smiths had sought
The Area Modern would be cheaper bought
But what rough friends at what a price
The ripe language was more than Mum could embrace,
A change to private school took place
With cousin Richard, gentler folk, more space
Here he grasped the needs of learning
But for University had no yearning
A farmer he would have to be
But no inheritance as he should have expected
An estate at least he could have contemplated
But death had erased such luxury from the scene
So a pauper now hard work to glean
Learn to farm by Jackaroo
In Norfolk to learn to till and sow

Raising animals their needs fulfil
Winter, tractor and plough and sow and till
Spring pride as lengthening green grain spread
This meant prosperous times ahead
This was the life for farmer Grahame
This is the life come sun, snow or rain
In summer, binder cut golden corn
To stack mid ribbledry and jesting born
In autumn, corn to sacks and barn
When finished sit around and yarn
Their job complete the year fulfilled
Harvest festivals, thanksgivings gild
And more great sacks flunk o'er strong back
And milk the cows a simple fact
Come frost and come the weather fair
This dependable lad he would be there
Well prepared his learning done
The next stage would not be so easy won
For sadly now there was no family farm
To inherit, the loss caused much alarm
The farm sold cheap cheap cheap quick in a 'diddle'?
A widow sad could not sought out this riddle
Valuable land sold cheap, in the war, in a fiddle?!
So off to Canada this flaxen haired, boy
To seek his fortune in farming employ
The salt smartened his face as ship's horn boomed
Excitement flamed his cheeks as the wind stormed.
Stepping to soil that he'd toil and tame
Blissful hope of fortune and pride his name
If he worked as hard as his poor father had to death
This fine young Englishman opportunity wreath
Take off to the Prairies on energy win

His fortune to make, come lets begin
A farmer doctor offered half share to run
His ranch midst hard work and fun
Soon his bride from UK came too
From which comfort and homelife flow
Hard work hardship times heat and cold in Water Valley
Fortitude, courage together they sally
Blessed with two darlings Richard and Dawn
Laughter and tiny feet lives adorn
They celebrated more up than down
For very soon they had a ranch of their own
The children flourished and fine kids they
But the marriage longevity did not obey
A cardiac virus cruel cut out the farm
His heart from heavy work take harm
Finally solution they both found
Grahame found new love in sweet Joanne bound
A solicitor of beauty, kindness, charm by loads
Restored domestic bliss in Calgary abode
She of immigrant farming Norwegian loyal
Some say Grahame's granny of Haakan royal
He by now had retrained in Land Estate Agency
And crop assessment when opportunity took fancy
Thereby make a change of tack
But a lot more comfort than farming, I'll back
But their happiness challenged by a fight with health
Cancer had rooted in Joanne with stealth
A fight to the core, tissue transplant accepted
And soon this scourge shewed signs of rejected
Their love for each other had greatly assisted
Restorance to health as hope joyous persisted
Grahame too had born since a child

Myopia extensive a bothering bile
Contact lenses, laser and eventual cataract extraction
Has given him final satisfaction
Now he can see points navigational
Which before were a trifle accidental
And now they smile in changed abode
In Victoria Vancouver Island explored
Bed and breakfast their latest whim
Giving Grahame lots of time to sail and swim?
Instead of gathering in the corn
He's burning the breakfast to laughter and scorn
He's acting and a father Christmas merry
And a fun Grandpa to adored young Wesley
His two own kids are happy with loves of their own
And accepts Joanne's brood as his and they're grown
With merry laughter joy and wit
To raise your glass is wondrous fit
God bless this family and all they do
And give them love and sunshine through

BMB-M

SWEET JAMIE

Sweet Jamie loved big children
And wanted so to play
This bouncy smiling loving one
Just two years old today
Two big boys took his tiny hands
And from his Mummie led
As she was paying for the bread
She momentarily dropped his hand
And off he tripped behind those boys
Hoping they'd soon shew him their lovely toys
And down the covered precinct
With bright shops on either side
His tiny legs could bare keep up
Big smile full of friendly pride
Out the door and down the road
Where lights were not so bright
He sudden looked around
His Mum was out of sight
He called her then and start to cry
Attracting attention from passers by
The boys by now were not so nice
His screaming loud brought loud rebuke
They hit him hard and down he fell
The tiny child was now so scared
He screamed the more
And fell on floor
The boys no more than 9 or 10
Gave him a kick to move again

A sweet old lady hearing the cries
Questioned the boys
Who brought forth lies
To the police station they were bent
They'd found the child with his head so dent
Anxious but accepting thus
She hastened off to catch her bus
Again and again he fell and stumbled
Whilst they pushed and kicked he tumbled
The next day the little treasure was found dead
On the railway line with crushed body and head
Train had upon this tender body tread
Dead from a crime most foul
To kill this innocent tiny soul
The world heard the news aghast
T.V. and press flooded the news full fast
The lady called the police that night
But given no priority as her wise words might
Perhaps if they'd acted he'd still be alive
And even tho' bruised he could have thrived
Video film had seen the three
So where were the culprits of this crime
Eventually found after long question time
From single mother homes these two
No father control over the savages new
A legacy of promiscuity and birth control pill
Men and women here there and everywhere
And never stay still
No real family life and discipline strong
For rough little tikes who to crime now belong
The liberalists are the true murderers
For they rebuke the schools that try
But can't use the cane or in courts they fry

Parents neither a good hearty slap
If caught they'll also be put on the mat
Joy riders from 10 years old
Laugh at the police who try to scold
65 offences and still running free
Is not unusual for under age spree
T.V and press are the real schools for crime
Freely available violence costing not a dime
Tiny James lays mourned and gone
Flowers on the spot to throng
His loving parents have lost their sweet treasure
This loss will be permanent loss beyond measure
God Bless his sweet soul for the angels to bear
To the Heaven for babes whilst we all shed a tear
Meanwhile
Drugs and crime now spread so fast
Law and order it cannot last
Shake up the media feed family clean
Take sex and violence from our scene
Both sexes need support of marriage strong
To nurture strong good people and to feel they belong
Sweep bad lads from the street
Into the army to sergeant major heat
Introduce God to clean their souls
For God has vanished from homes and schools
Crack in the discipline
Clean the street
To save the innocents
Make civilisation complete

BMB-M

One man's delight is another man's curse

Why has science not attended to mens needs
When unwanted and unloved feeds cursed deeds
Into war crime violence rape abuse
Where is the relief to this defuse
Science manly problems does neglect
His comfort should focus urgent affect
As the antidote or instrument gains peace
For many freedom and longevity the lease
Males from puberty to grave
Men need this new relief
Mankind to save

BMB-M

A GUERNSEY YOUTH ORCHESTRA

A teacher came to test
Our children's aptitude for strings
When in July '74
We dwelt upon another aspect of these things
"Was a Guernsey Youth Orchestra in existence?"
I did quizzically enquire
"Sadly, not" replied Miles Attwell
"If you wish, proceed
I promote you to inspire"
Knowing not quite how to start
To help bring forth this feat
The Victoria Road Eye Clinic
We offered for interested folk to meet
Admixing medicines, microscopes and contact lenses
With concertos, cantatas and cadenzas
At a Beechwood concert an announcement
Did this same teacher contribute
Which we followed by a meeting
Letters sanctioned to distribute
To music teachers at all the schools
And those in education
To musically minded parents
And those of no musical vocation
The meeting of December 5th 1974
Permitted a formed committee
Promote the idea more
Education department, teachers, parents, all
Aired views at this occasion

Amid a breezy squall
Kind Reuben Dorey
Diverted much dissention
This Youth Orchestra
Was our immediate intention
Four years later
We've our purpose achieved
A political positive
And all so relieved
The enlightened States
Voted a Youth Music "Yes"
With four music salaries
To support the music quest
Now dear children
Acclaim with gratitude
Express with hard practice
And perfectionist attitude
Remember Bill Rowe
A violin teacher well renowned
Remember Louis Guillemette
Who we all greatly mourned
Remember Pere Lecluze
Whose interest helped keep the quest alive
These three, chaired well their good committees
Made policy to thrive
Remember John Stephenson
In States Education
Who quietly supported
The idea to maturation
Remember Cyril Hockaday
And his happy Brass Band
Who further drove the project

For this tiny patch of land
Remember Mrs Guillemette
Amid whose coffee morning quorum
A ladies' committee, we stood up and formed
At a publicising forum
Remember Jenny Swainston, and these ladies
Who worked so long and hard
To swell funds for music instruments
And the grand idea to guard
Remember all the teachers
Who taught the strings so small
Miles Atwell, Lynn de Guerin, Meg Cresswell
And others, patient in their call
Remember the musical schools
Who gave of time and space
Running excellent courses
Better standards to embrace
Remember Dame Ruth Railton
Who the NYO had founded
Gave, here in 1976
Time, expense, energy unbounded
Remember Mrs Wheeler
The Parkinsons
Dr Saumarez's
Ethertons
Spittals
Opening their houses free
For funds to purchase music instruments
To loan without a fee
Remember all the excellent performers
Who practised long for their perfection
Without whose efforts

There'd be no funds
For musical distribution
They gathered pennies for every Guernsey child
A YOUTH ORCHESTRA in mind
All the work that this involved
It was indeed most goodly kind
Remember Mr Aeschimann
Who gave a generous sum
Remember dear young Le Cocq whose life passed
But barely begun
To all good folk unmentioned
Who helped in any way
To give the project a forward push
And prevent its down decay
Shew your gratitude you youngsters
In your attitude to work
Shew to all these dear good folk
That you'll your discipline never shirk
We have our Mr Wormesley
A peripatetic full in action
Conducting our New Youth Orchestra
Formed for music satisfaction
That committee originated
Four whole years ago
Continues to promote
These origins to flow
Friends of the Youth Orchestra
It is newly named
The Youth Orchestra is now a States affair
And thus of them acclaimed
What a tremendous effort
For an end achieved so excellent well

We wish unlimited years of happiness
Beauteous sounds our shores to swell
Alert young tooters and scrapers
Dispense with the vapours
You've someone to beat with his baton
Clever and not so
Rich and Poor
If you play an instrument
Follow that law
All equal in an orchestra
In this our self-made fun
Let's blast on the trumpet
And thunder on the drum
A St Stephen's Concert inaugural
On the 18th March
They've practised for months
Without hysteria or starch
This wonderful era
Has just begun
We anticipate decades
Of musical fun
Stand up ye youngsters
Get up and cheer
We'll expect marvellous music
For many a year.
I thank all these folk
Who made my dream come true
For it would never have come about
Without the help from you

BMB-M

SPRING IN LAMPETER

In a narrow lane in Lampeter
As it drizzles with rain on my windscreen
The first swallows dart like arrows
As I drive, they are hardly seen
Speed of lightening
Scooping up insects
About turn in mid air
On the wing
All swiftly, sleekly silently
For only when nesting
Has one heard them sing
The tall yarram like poised confetti
The chick weed sprinkled in the grass
The dandelions thick bright and bold
Make sunshine even when its grey and cold
The May blossom pure fresh wellcome
The oak leaves yellow to green
The sycamore stretching its infant leaves
The hedges clipped, smart and clean
Like linear well shorn sheaves
Tended for centuries with variety alive
Until the advent of modern machinery
Upon these the hedger's families thrive
Protecting traffic from the straying flock
And protecting the farmer from losing stock
Curving traversing the pasture
With sleek artistic lines
Dividing sculpted shapes

Of quilted patchwork kind
As far into the distance
The deep hedge scrolls a line
But even to the mile
The shape we can define
Protecting herds of calving Friezians
And sheep that care for lambs
These never ending hedges
And the grass within their walls
Are the security fodder of the farmer
Upon which the plight of tables
Upon his skill and planning
Is the bread upon our plate
Upon the hedgerows grass and farmer
Depend our stomachs to be sate.

As the trees stretch tall in green meadows
And the lambs skip hither in play
The buzz of the tractor engine
Is loudly having its say
All manner of birds in the mating
Kites and buzzards on the wing
And mother leads troops of ducklings
In the stream that leaps from the spring
Nature bursts with excitement
Let daisies and buttercups join hands and sing
Sunshine blossom and dance in a ring
Happy Happy Happy Spring.

BMB-M

LEARN TO BE A MAN OF GOD

Blustering buffoon
Egotistical man of straw
Why do you open
Then slam the door
To be a man of your word
Is a beacon of light
Make no promises you cannot keep
Never anticipate
Where you cannot leap
For a man of God is sure and strong
His word is his bond
And his kindness long

BMB-M

CHILDREN OF BESLAM

We weep with the angels
A huge cloud blotted out the sun
As 100 sweet children of Beslam
At school
Were extinguished by bomb and by gun
An indescribable hell was in Russia
Of devils that took these sweet lives
Religious hatred engendered this horror
And barely a child survives
Now the whole world weeps with the angels
As gently we coax to life
Some lucky parent's little ones
The few injured who survive.

BMB-M

LADDER OF LOVE

Climb the ladder of love to Heaven
As we step the dance of bliss
Look into my eyes
And seal this Heaven
With a kiss
Anxieties melt and vanish
Weaving magic such as this
Look into my eyes
Seal this Heaven with a kiss

BMB-M

Promiscuity unhimges civilisation

An affront to ones maker
When women indulge
When at ease with free-love
They brag to divulge
An insult to the precious
Womb of their babes
Should be total exclusive
Civilisation to save
Should be proud to be thus
Otherwise life is disgust
Dignity flees
And problematic disease
Stand exclusive and straight
And example to make
Thus society to build
Strong walls not to break

B.M.B-M.

YELLOW FIELDS

Everywhere bright yellow
Fields are seen
Yellow flowers to yellow margarine
Nourishing the nation
With polyunaccharides
To stop heart attacks and strokes
And a multitude besides
Health
Health
Proceed with stealth
For life is too short
Listen to each statistic
Read every report

BMB-M

MOTHER CHRISTMAS

Lonely Grans and grandpas do not cry
Mother Christmas passes by
You will have this Christmas Day
All your sweet old heart could pray
Feast and Friendship Town Hall Fun
Dry your tears its just begun
Families come with smiles and food
And put you in the party mood
Muff up with your coat and hat
Switch off fires and feed the cat
A car outside to take you there
And lovely folk who really care
Carol, tinsel trimmings tree
Cheerful friendly company
Turkey, puddings, presents sweets
And lots of fun and Christmas treats
Happy Happy Christmas Day
Because mother Christmas passed your way

BMB-M

SNOW SPRINKLED MOUNTAINS

Wales
I must visit the snow sprinkled mountains
Where the peaks inscribe clouds in the sky
Sunny cirrus and thunderous cumulous
Where singing skylarks poise, dive and fly
Where racing streams rumble, roar and swell
Then to thin silver ribbon- to heaven from hell
Where shivering lambs to their mother's heels stay
Until they are bigger when with other babes play
Where mists, white swirling mysterious
Lop the mountains round to square
Fierce winds whistle fury
Quiet sunsets pink orange flare
They are moody these magnificent mountains
Full emotions liberally spread
Unrepressed, unrepentant surpising
A beautiful rainbow ahead 14.2.90

BMB-M

ENIGMA

Life is an enigma
With paths like spokes of a wheel
Which one shall we take
With how much zest and zeal
Some they may destroy us
And some weave sunshine warm
Our characters will hopefully lead us
Away from ones of harm
Our instincts to pursue the good
Will find those pathways safe and clear
Protect us on life's complex routes
Compass set miss strife and fear 17.1.97

BMB-M

PURE SOUL

It is around this heavenly twine
That we seek of thee and thine
A soul that's pure and fine and free
That fills with awe the likes of me
A soul that floats on cobweb light
Always daylight
Never night
Full of spring and love and smiles
Never mingling negative guiles
Oh come dear Soul around us wrap
Toss away our foolish frap
Let us be as light and free
Abundant kind and good as thee
Then we'll be as rainbow flowers
Celestial music throughout the hours
Laughing children kind at play
And sunshine bright eternal day
Oh come sweet Spirit influence mine
That I may stretch for the divine

BMB-M

TIDE'S RIGHT FOR A SAIL IN GUERNSEY.

Quick
Quick
Pack the lunch
Add the drinks and add the punch
Dress ye quick and off and away
The tide's right and we're sailing today
Untidy warm clad lot
Scramble aboard the tilting yacht
Hold tight heave up safe
We don't want thee a wet wee waif
Put on them jackets to save your life
Now no grumbles 'cos we don't want strife
The winds rattling halliards loud
Tide's right and we're a happy crowd
O.K, let go that rope we're off and away
Laughing faces enjoying the spray
Heave up the mainsail, fix the jib
We're out of the wind so give engine a flip
Soon we're out and over the shelf
Away from the lea of the marina's stealth
Out amongst the bobbing boats
Out in the wind we tighten our coats
Avoiding the moorings of those out of hail
Who left much earlier for a sail
Hi watch it a moment, let us go first
For the open ocean we've acquired a great thirst

Big booming mail boats indicate round we must
In order to avoid being inextricably trussed
And towed to Weymouth against our will
Unbeknown to them on the bridge, at the till'
Never mind soon out of the Harbour and into the swell
Good! its blowing hard and blowing well
A good force 4 and the lapping we hear
Bracing and balancing, never a fear
Hurray it's fun, the day's bright
The wind's good
And the tide's right.
We're off for a sail

BMB-M

TWO LITTLE INNOCENTS CHRISTMAS SHOPPING AT BOOTS IN ST PETER PORT

Two little innocents in the big Boots store
Hand in hand shopping in the ground and first floor
Aged 8 and 9 in the big wide world to spend
Was Emma and Anne Marie her little friend
Five single pounds each folded tight
Excited, independent, eyes large and bright
Mamma before departing instructed them attend
The main door entrance, when finished shopping
Each with her little friend
Alone with too many folk crowding all around
Hands and purses clutched tightly
Little hearts afflutter found
Then to make for the counter for the business in hand
We'll get no shopping done if on this spot we longer stand
Each critically assessed each lovely thing
As suitable or not before cash register ring
Several people's ages and tastes in mind
Several special presents to search and find
Each thing discussed and carefully merits weighed
Before rejected or a purchase made
Voices low incase recipients got a clue
Once purchased hastily in the bag and out of view
Heads close, purse held tightly gripped
Bag kept closed, decisions tight lipped
Well aware a pickpocket might be near

Taking excellent precautions against that ghastly fear
Daddy said pipe cleaners would be very nice
If only they could find them that would be suffice
Mamma said a pencil with a rubber at the end
Would be a lovely gift   her heart to rend
For sisters three something fun or of strong perfume
Would excellently well fulfill the tune
And the dear little lady who lives
In the cottage by the church
Aunty Margaret would appreciate
A lovely talcum powder search
The money was dwindling as the pounds replaced by coins
For frequent counts, two heads in concentration join
Even a penny short in change was respectfully queried
Before continuing satisfied down the counters oh, so varied
Fearing separation holding hands
Rather tiny on tip toe stand
Watching the clock with care and attention
Not wanting to be late
For the meeting of Ma's mention
At last all presents bought
All perfection, lovingly sought
So many big and pushy people
To try to get past
Not much time so they'd have to be fast
Clutching purse and presents bought
To the door they hastily fought
Big pushy people nearly made them drop the bag
Their pounding little hearts did a mighty sag
But the right door at last was thankfully found
And triumphantly they looked eagerly around
And there Mamma's were smiling

At their successful daughters feat
With obvious relief the tiny shoppers to greet
Horrah these mites had their project completed
Now a drink and a bun somewhere warm
Their anxious tums to be repleted.

BMB-M

NAILS AND HOOFS!

The lady's weaponry does consist
Not of the foot and not of the fist
But the right thumbnail spruce and long
Well pointed tough and strong
When her bossy little classmate
Did urge this child to concentrate
Up went the hackles the nail pressed hard
Into the palm of the friends left hand
Amid much alarm
Friend was less covert in her inflicted sin
It was out with the foot and into the shin
Then its tales of woe to Daddy tearfully remitted
Much accentuated effect by bruise on leg affected
But no mention of her naughty nail
That was plunged asunder in our tale.
Now come little girls this really is not kindly
To change your ways you really must find
Never thump back that which is given
Or you'll never get to Heaven
Sensitivity and quick alarm
Is the attitude that ignites the harm
Instead pull a face of kindly hurt
And the friend will be sorry for her remarks so curt
So with apologies, patience kindness and strength
A friendship grows to greater length

BMB-M

THE SEIGNEUR'S SONS EVENTUALLY MAKE THE QUEEN'S VISIT TO SARK

The Seigneur's sons set out for Sark
With the Queen and the Duke to make their mark
But the weather with mist and fog was spoiled
And their attempted landing at Guernsey was foiled
The pilot then to Dinard diverted
With the Seigneur's sons most disconcerted
An impossible plight
This diverted flight
Due in Sark at eleven next day forseen
To be presented to the Duke and the Queen
The B-M's with whom they were to have stayed
Set out to undo the mess that was made
British Airways could not tell
To which hotel their fate befell
Dear dear what could they do?
No hotel to send messages to
This clue it must be sorted
Or the new attempt be firmly aborted
So off to the airport for confrontation
Set off this friend with determination
A pilot responded to persuasive please!
And gave the hotel with relative ease
Now who had a boat, who was next to be sought
For transport from Guernsey to Sark was the thought
From Dinard to Guernsey just possibly might

Be made by twin engined smaller flight
Now, who did we know who knew the boys too
Who'd be kind enough to see them through?
The answer was the Dorey's the Condor chief
And a request granted, with great relief
It solved not Guernsey to Sark
But from Dinard to Guernsey made its mark
The boat from St Malo at 7 leaving
Next morning to Jersey and Guernsey arriving
To find seats
Quick to the phone
But she was answered "sorry none"
But surely a hundred seats to fill
Someone bound to be ill
She went away to have a thought
Returning, said "two could be bought"
Well, well only part but must accept them smart
"Would you accept payment at the Jersey end?"
Was the question now posed by this friend
"No sorry" was the quick reply
"That would not acceptably with the rules comply"
"But suppose the Condor Chief did allow
Will you reverse this obstacle now?"
In reply to this our guess
Her reply was "definitely yes"
However, in 10 mins she would from duty be gone
So speed imperative on the phone
Luckily Peter Dorey was quickly found
He telephoned Condor in St Malo making firm ground
He did the seats to Guernsey secure
To make the aim so much more sure
Now, to see if the boys had arrived

Hotelled where the pilot had surmised
Indeed they were there and listened intent
"Be up at 6 " if to Sark they were bent
"Hurrah!" they said, " then's not all in vain"
"We'll be up at dawn and take the strain"
There was another factor yet
That had to be solved e're success beget
The harbour Master's advice was sought
How from Guernsey to Sark
In ½ hour could be brought

A very fast launch would thus be the need
He'd find a person for this deed
This he did both quick and efficient
A person of boat, speed and proficient
So back on the phone the boys to tell
"The journey back to Sark should now go well"
I'd slaved for our friends and now rest reposed
And hope go as supposed
Indeed it did
Up at dawn on hydrofoil
Change at Jersey and to Guernsey the foils to toil

Arriving but 10 mins only late
And excellent efficient met them at the gate
Off to Sark at 30 knots to dart
Changing clothes whilst bumping
They must be smart
Thumping and swerving the rocks to evade
In a mere twenty minutes their journey made
The grand Brittania dressed over all was standing
When at Maseline Harbour they made their landing

Up the Sark hill red faced they panted
To keep ahead of the Queen's coach
For now she had landed
Now they took a short cut to ease
The Royal party went to the hall for Chief Pleas
Here for the Seigneur to to vow allegiance
Under the dignitaries surveillance
The boys rushed on all sweating and worn
Too late for their father's oath to see
But might glimpse the Queen at the Seignerie
The Queen, Duke and Seignerie parents were then to arrive
As the boys triumphant at the back door dive
And all did meet with such delight
The parents much relieved at their sons sight
Their story to all they did relate
How from Dinard to Sark did make
If doubt of Royal allegiance you ever find
Just bring this tale into your mind 6.77

BMB-M

THE DRAIN TRAIN

They are most polite on the drain train
They queue in elaborate style
In a way that's especially English
In strictly parallel style
Forming a pattern of neat cross hatching
Headed where the doors just should be
No touch of the sleeve nor shoving
As polite as ever you'd see
It's used by those gentlemen from the big banks
But economy reflects but minimal thanks
Shuttling down to Bank from Waterloo
This migratory flight full to overflow
The obedient little train back and forth it shuffles
The long suffering driver his boredom he muffles
He thinks his own thoughts while they pack in tight
And shunts back and forth from morn 'til night
Two great bands of activity he observes
When the banks flex and relax their nerves
In the morning at nine and quarter too
The evening at 5 back to Waterloo
A band in the morning and a band at night
The drain train groans under the migratory flight.

BMB-M

JACK THE GENTLEMAN FARMER

Jack had fought diphtheria
Which this cricketers strength had sapped
He was due to study Classics at Oxford
But his physicians this plan had capped
You are a landowner enjoy that life
The dust and poor life at Oxford
Would cause your health strife.
Reluctant this 6 foot 3 handsome man
Agreed to a u-turn in his plan
A year on Jonty Slater's Farm
In Somerleyton agriculture calm
Far cry from academic paper
But fun and more so a gentlemanly caper
Labourers to do the nasty chores of farming
Occasional point to point spills
The most alarming
Social life in much demand
This charming man
Courtly in command
For a man so academic bright
Hardly Oxford
But the horse and gun he liked
From his steward he took Holly Farm Barnby over
Horsemen, cowmen, hedgers and ditchers to cover
A beauty Margaret he adored and married
Blessed with six infants she joyously carried
All was fine 'til 39
When Hitler and war did undermine

To his father's estate he took his brood further
Far from bombs to White House Farm Rumburgh
Jack's spats and britches were covered in mud
His boots full deep in the dung
For a gentleman farmer whose life had been smooth
His life now seemed dismal and done
Bridge, shooting and horses and point to point courses
A memory of past gone fun
Hitler's army had threatened and from England had drained
Healthy young labourers
And left landowners sick and maimed
To work cows and horses and sickle and scythe
To raise food to keep England alive
Poor Jack was not strong
A lean 6 foot 3 long
Not built for the CWT sack
Not bent to the sickle or scythe did he know
Nor harnessing Suffolks to plough straight and sow
Nor sat on the roller
Nor with binder to mow
Nor following the drill
The heavy soil sow
What the labourers had previously done
Was left alas to a struggling son
Spring leaves flowers and sunshine and gentle soft breeze
Seemed brief and soon gone
Leaving deep mud and freeze
The pretty hedgerows with colour alive
Willow green and swallow dive
The joys of harvest
When shocks of gold corn
Were borne on wagon to stockyard

On days long and warm
Mid happy young family drenched in the sun
But soon threshing was finished
And winter soon come
The rain drenched and soaked and cloud overbrewed
And the etched winter landscape his strength n'er embued
But Margaret's home cooking delicious and plenty
Made sure the family's plates were never empty
16th century mod cons meant candles and cold
But great fires and warm clothes fought the damp and the mould
Always a cheerful hardworking lady
Little help, as was used to, as war did destable
Jack found cows slow and stubborn jostling on frost hardened mud
Couldn't care who had slaved so they could chew on the cud
Unaware of their benefactor cutting hay high sway on the stack
As the East wind chilled his bones, with a sack on his back
Cows milked by hand with his head in the flank
In a cow nettice lonely, cold dark eerie and dank
Water pumped up and carried to scrub buckets and mess
Left by the cows including Elsie and Bess
The milk to be cooled churned and carted up long lonely drive
All slaving to keep England's millions alive
The beet to be cut then carted to feed
The grooming harnessing great horses to heed
The crops to be hoed and hedges trimmed low
The leaks to be stopped and rat traps to know
One man doing the work of a dozen before
Was heartbreak depleting unenviable chore
Up in all weathers at the crack of dawn
A sack on his back and stifling a yawn
A wonderful wife and demanding 5

None quite old enough to help all to thrive
Jack's strength it did dwindle
This sparse young spindle
He perished a victim of war
Hitler could add Jack to his score
Overwhelming work outrageous
He dealt with most courageous
For Jack in mid winter
Crushed beneath demands of the land
Dear Jack with pneumonia could no longer stand
Sick and anxious for his beloved and five
Fought with strength but did not survive
His grave lies in Suffolk his land all around
This brave 35 year old in his final patch of ground
His grave lies in Barnby Churchyard amid his green fields
O'er which the seasons clock o'er steals
But no medals mark this particular brave
Who gave his life dear England to save
If only to Oxford he had gone
Instead of a slave he'd have been a don

Jack Barnard 1908-1943.

BMB-M

SPRING

Cirrus clouds scudding
Across the clear blue sky
Viewed behind confetti
Swaying banks of parsley high
Edging the sunshine golden
Field of mustard nigh
Perfumed prior to
Later summer's yield
When apple blossom
Excites one's visual sense
Spring at its height
Exquisite joy immense

BMB-M

BEECH GROVE

Sweet beeches reach towards the sky
From root to tip a hundred feet high
A group of 4 their mingling leaves
As branches and twigs a basket weaves
Shady, dense and cool embowered
Grassy neath is rarely showered
Sheep there cluster snuggling close
Where cool companionship muster most
As grasses tall wave in the breeze
And blazing summer scatters seeds
As poppies bright and foxgloves bend
Sweet daisies at their feet extend
Buttercups dainty waft and play
As swallows dart and speed display
Skylarks flutter sing on high
Blackbirds and thrushes teach young to fly
From nests within this complex haven
Within this beech grove leaves a laden
Beauteous grand great height and span
Grandly mid quite spacious land
Glorious sculpture priceless antique
What greater beauty could you seek 3.7.89

BMB-M

PICNIC SPOT

Here in tranquil picnic spread
With cotton fluff and blue o'er head
We wonder at these trees great might
Amid broad landscape cornfield bright
What matters more than this to save
From Prescott concrete jungle's harsh pervade
For this is centuries of tender care
The best of nature and man's best flair

BMB-M

HISTORIC BRICKWALL FARMHOUSE

14-15th century

When England was yet young in years
This house was shelter for joy, love tears
With gentle landscape infinite well it blends
Linking close the centuries of farming craft it tends
Gently do its ancient timbered walls
Gaze upon open fields with seasons changing calls
The winters blue grey frosty green
With pheasants bright their feathers gleam
In spring with twittering birds excited
Fresh green grass so bright ignited
With daffodils primroses cowslips yellow
The cold hard earth has turned more mellow
The crops beneath the winter's soil
Turns green then gold
And then's the toil
For centuries labourers
Diagonal scythes in line
Work corner to corner
To reap the corn in time
Then flail the wheat and barley oats
To loose the grain
For bread and porridge, beer
Their nourishment to gain
Later binder through the leaded panes seen
The sheaths to shocks and wagons glean
The rabbit chase and children fun

The harvest race to catch the sun
Now combine harvester with infinite ease
But no comraderie of summer's lease
The wise oaks stare they've seen it all
As ash and sycamore; elms now hardly seen at all
This tranquil place with hollyhocks at the door
Moorhen chasing duck from ponds fine store

Nooks and cranies
Timber daub and wattle
Rooms here and there
Grandpas at the bottle
Little maids in white
Frilly apron and cap
One has a baby on her lap

The smelly tramp drops by
And terrified children hide
He shuffles to the kitchen door
Given a hot cup of tea
And fresh cookies galore
The backhouse boy leads him on his way
To shuffle his poor existence
For another day

As snow piles hedges
The plague brought tears
And all ages folk to die
Good souls lifted
To their place on high
Sweet children, fathers mothers all affected
Sometimes no person left

The place neglected
Or maybe lucky
Praise in prayers
To live this life
A few more years

The priest shakes nervous
In his hole beneath the roof
After furtive Mass
With wine and loaf
The King's men tap the
Timbers with their swords
In this Catholic house
As they search the boards
But well camouflaged this secret hide
Priest hole protects 'til they're safe outside
King Henry to Catholics so cruel
Traitors gave the soldiers fuel

Queen Mary crosses the moat safe and sound
As galloping to castle Framlingham ground
Sits regal at table whilst courtiers low bow
Soon refreshed with good food and away fast now
Enemies are close farewell goodbyes
Her Majesty left to much relieved sighs
Danger beckons in fragile times
Bolt doors, stay close and hope God is kind

Children cuddle dogs and cats
And rescue frightened rabbit
Slide down stacks and hide in hay
Swing on willows is their habit

Stroke great Suffolk horses strong
As pull heavy wagon or plough along
Pat the cows as the milk maids make revelry now
Tease the children with a squirt of milk from the cow
They race out to mother's call to sumptuous cooking smells
"We're coming now we're starving "
The sturdy children yell
Clean faces to the table
As quick as you are able
Enjoy your food my children all
Or you'll never grow up to be strong and tall

These happy creaking timbers
Six whole centuries held their might
Kept out the cold and in the light
Countless years held families warm
Who trod the floors and up at dawn
New born babes draw first breath within these doors
Children's voices echo on the three floors
Mothers anxious fed their flock
As caring fathers tend the stock

Christmas happy stockings fill
Christenings, weddings birthdays still
Alas, eventual prime doth meet decline
E'en where the care is excellent fine
Old age or ill last breath inhale
Last tearful journey to the Church entail
The saddened home still drying tears
From when England was yet young in years
I close my eyes and imagine centuries past

Sweet children laughing at Inglenook hearth
A merry throng at table laden
Enjoy God's food in this safe haven
A quip a tease
A laugh a sneeze
Then to bed with candles bright
To sleep like angels through the night
This wondrous warm and lovely house
Unfounded fears it'll not arouse
It sleeps and wakes its timbers calm
Soothing and protecting from all harm
Bursting with memories of ancient ages
Happiness and sadness upon life's pages
When England was yet young in years
This house sheltered joy, love, tears

BMB-M

TUMMIES AND SPIRITS

Sweet good religion of diverse forms
Why seek ye not to quell starvation's storms?
For here lies human deprivation raw
Step from the pulpit and disperse from store
Spend not your time in scheming forth ambition
Climbing the next rung to hierarchy fruition
Instead, seek ye to fulfill not only spirit's needs
But ensure those starving folk have all their feeds
Therein lies truer good
Such as Christ us taught
Low is the spirit
If the body of such lack
Is fraught

BMBMBM

THE CHICKEN SALE

The best feathered hens
Form the basis of this tale
They were a sample of 12 such
Intended for the sale
Penned up, proud and squawking loud
Necks craned because they never saw before
Such pretty things for auctioning
Arriving by the score
They'd had so much attention
Manners impeccable
Worth a mention
At last!
After an interminable wait
Whilst they fluffed their feathers
And strutted their gait
Up climbed the auctioneer bristling smart
Most competent and able
To conduct the Forest mart
The auction got upon its way
The hammer went down often
Some delight and some dismay
The hens preened again their feathers
Feeling their impending turn
For the fall of the hammer
Wondering how much they would earn
All this for the Forest Church
Unknown fate
Table or perch

Their feathers were quivering
At the contrast in choice
They'd very soon know
Whether to cry or rejoice
They'd gone off their laying
It was very well known
For three year olds they were
Plump and well grown
'Twas this fact that made them unstable
Could be the bidder would arrange stuff and table
Whilst these thoughts passed their tormented minds
The auctioneer chanted his well versed lines
"Come now my friends a dozen frisky feathered hens
Hand bred on the best corn that Guernsey pretends
Free range
Pecking at the most selective weeds
And sneaking flowers and vegetables
According to their needs
Come now regard these fat feathered beauties
Nearing the end of laying, I can't deny
But to find better beasts I'd you defy
Come now a bid to start proceedings
Give a good price to justify their feedings"
Not a whisper!
Not a sound !
No hand movement, no wink or grimace
From the earlier hilarity and din
Suddenly one could hear a pin
" Come on me hearties
Lets have a start
Lets have a good price
At the Forest Mart"
He charmed and persuaded but never a spark
To pluck those poor chucks would not be a lark

For that activity they had no flair
Thought the many timid bidders there
No stomach for the preliminaries to do
Before the plucking was even in view
Sudden vegetarianism swept though the hall
Those chucks to the table had no culinary call
And after a lengthy pause
Down came the hammer
"No bids for this cause"
The hens not fully realizing a significant release
Started to squawk and squawk without cease
The bidders assumed it was triumphant relief
They were thrilled not to envisage
The table of grief
But no!
Crest fallen, rejected sadly left out
They'd have preferred the table
To total doubt
Their ego deprived
Their feathers marred
Their morale permanently scarred
Their kindly master, relieved, retorted
"Keep your pecker up
I'll take you home and give you your sup
My feathered beauties you've have had a reprieve
Stop squawking and this auction we'll leave
So calm your egos and we'll give a donation
And promise to lay in your next location
If your eggs drop off ever again
Its off to the auction and into the pen
Now no more squawking
I was only joking!" 1977

BMB-M

THE EVERLASTING CURRIDGE COTTAGE ROSE
IN MEMORY OF GEOFFREY AND MAY SHAW

This rose came from the cottage
Retiring did here dwell
Geoffrey Shaw did all the pruning
And Gran did water well
Pale pink blooms in great profusion
Great length and breadth it spanned
Fence hidden in seclusion
Air gently perfumed fanned

Their daughters took a cutting
With gentle care to flourish
And soon another fence to clothe
More family eyes to nourish
That dear enfolded, sweet, sweet rose
Of such determination
Did serve to give such great delight
To another generation

And now I take another twig
To plant it in the ground
With love and care I'll make it grow
'Til flowers there are around
For we're the third and ours the fourth
Generations are a casting

To give delight that's heaven sent
A rose that's everlasting 1977 Guernsey

BMB-M

ALL SLOG AND SLUM AT OXFORD UNIVERSITY -AMID WORLD CLASS EDUCATION

Exquisite spires and sanctuary gardens
Chapel music bliss celestial
Beautiful sandstone ancient buildings
Libraries well ordered and finest intellectual

But
Raw and callous is Oxford
A slum culture feigning as best
No place for gentle students
Blinkered hard tutors seek no redress

A Godforsaken frenetic survive-if-you-can philosophy
Chasing essays the whip lashing time piece
No college soft furnishings or flowers fresh
Vampire landlords for slums, students fleece

Bare and hard is Oxford
Only libraries given much grace
Students scorned faceless money grab commodities
To keep tutors and books in this place

Eight weeks of unmitigated misery, course and harsh
No place of home comfort the student find
Frenzied bareboard or live out slum
Leave memories of domestic squalor grind

Is there no-one who cares for their welfare
Only attention to paper and books
These are civilized beings flung into Oxford
All slum and slog are its looks
They need:
Spacious soft fresh flowered sitting rooms with kindly attendants
In every college and in central Oxford provide
Which at their peril each student respects
There home life a glimmer resides

Shame on shambolic Oxford
Of Chapels exquisite fine
Spending liberally on Choristers Church music
Whilst students live like swine

Where are the biweekly plays and concerts
Free for students to take and nourish
Fragmented education for the elite
Will not make our country flourish

Weekly warm dinner parties for 12 formal
Sponsors: town, gown, government, industry impart
To host kindly civilized idea exchange
To engender a civilized heart

Now put your "workhouse" in order Oxford
Personal requirements must attention be given
Laundry cleaning women and comfort
Maybe mothers turn this hell into Heaven

Scandalous deprivation in Oxford
As young ladies and gentlemen should
In learning demeanor intellectual and living
Training of top brains and good

Then light the candle of comfort
And give warmth a chance to win through
Oxford is a historic ghetto
Not a place for gentle civilized to go

BMB-M

DOWN WIND FROM A CIGARETTE
Stoneleigh Station

Beautiful air of a clear, tingling, fresh, cool strain
As I wait on the platform
For the Waterloo train
Few pollutants in this Stoneleigh air there are
For its yet too early for the commuter's motor car
And yet as I'm giving my facial skin a treat
My nostrils are suddenly some acridity to meet
I am absolutely in the down wind standing
And that offensive garbage is upon me full square landing
The offender knows not that he does thus tar
My pure respiring lungs from afar
His efforts of such suicide intention
Will no doubt need future medication
And it has a look most comical
And quite the reverse of economical
And it so much detracts from dignity and grace
The strange little cylinder placed within the face.

BMB-M

DARLING CHILD FULL OF FUN

Darling little one full of fun
Tousled all over hair undone
Come for a cuddle, come for a kiss
For when you're grown
That's what I'll miss

Bring your soft bunny
Cuddle te dum
Snuggle under the blankets
And cover your tum
We won't get dressed yet
Of meals we'll forget
I'll find your favourite page in
Winnie the Pooh
I'll play Piglet and Eeyore
Just for you
Sweet bubbling eyes all sparkling with fun
What a delicious life you've just begun

BMB-M

JAZZY JOCTOR

Dear Dr Geoff what a surprise we find
Under the G.P. of a most conventional kind
What is it that you really like?
A piano, a band and a receptive mike
The improvising beat striking gentle soft and clear
Modern jazz of a very haunting air
Little did the multitude waiting their turn
Realise their doctor had a secret yearn
To produce beating music in a smoky haze
Until exhausted in a happy daze
Sometimes the trumpeter takes the light
Then the drummer thunders his plight
Now the piano's turn to take the sway
Each follows other no gaps nor delay
None too much of his own bent
Each to the other the limelight lent
My! But what refreshment really good
What a release from the medical flood
How good a contrast from neurotic moaning
Of the discontent the injections the phoning
Paper work that's high in piles
Sudden emergencies, medical files
Bureaucratic surplus meetings
Of overpaid vacuous idle leechings
The family boggle delighted at the sight
Delectable sounds into the night
Proud of father's new found versatility
De dum de dum de dum
Delightful audibility

BMB-M

LAMBS ON THE HILLSIDE

Over the trout stream that ripples in flow
Where recently icicles mingled with snow
Up winding roads where the trees stand bare
But stately in expectancy stretched high to fresh air
In soft green turf nestle daffodils and snowdrops
Nodding approval in the soft green balm
For there thro' the hedgerow they've spied spring's new joy
Each ewe watchful of her delicious fluffy toy
Each new lamb like a leggy rabbit leaping
Fluffy white dots on the hillside all ableating
Cluster as playmates and then run off to mum
Hither and thither 'til the night takes o'er from sun
As dusk pervades the grassland
The lambs stray not from ewe
The flock is close and guarded
'Til the sunrise and the dew
And then the lambs will sprinkle
The green with joy and life
To frollick in a fresh new day
That shepherd frees from strife

BMB-M

WOMEN CLEANERS AT THE BANK

Happy women cleaners cackling crowding at the stone
From which this grandiose bank was hewn
Lively cockney humour shrieks and slaps abound
They've finished all their sweeping and scrubbing of the ground
No particular respect for the building grand
At the banking centre of the land
Out steps a man in black so crisp so smart
Cold in his homberg, maybe hiding warmer heart
In fitting with this edifice so fine and so tall
But such a contrast to these cackling ladies all
Who laugh and sway in happy fun
So thankful that their arduous day is done

BMB-M

KINDLY WORK WITH THE ELDERLY AT PLAS PADARN WALES

Fly over Plynlimmon
To the curve over Cardigan Bay
Where the ocean lifts and falls
And the curlews wheel and play
Where the Dovey lakes then snakes
And the sheep so peaceful graze
Where the land rises to the sky
And mountains recede blue in the haze
Close by this isolated population
Did St Padarn establish his foundation
In the depth of centuries past
Maintaining souls who for our God
Practised prayer, self denial and fast
Over the knoll peeked by warrior acclaim
Wellingtons column has tranquil lain
Lies the peaceful and impressive church
Of Llanbadarn strong and still
On that same monastic hill
Is a beautiful house of great delight
At sunset blazing in light so bright
Guarded by two eagles and a garden sublime
Where the monks maybe sung their vespers
In their Godliness divine
Here now is a refuge for the frail and old
Drawn in from misery loneliness and cold
To be cosseted and fed with gentle care

By angels of goodness and wholesome fare
Problems smoothed and from despair erased
Lovingly helped and life rephrased
Heavy responsibility and draining heavy work
From which no kindly employee would ever shirk
This is a place of grace a place most kind
Which is a haven for the hopeless old
No better ever find

BMB-M

DISASTER AT ALFROQUES

European children spritely in fun
The holidays had just begun
Splashing in the water
Basking in the sun
Laughing and playing
Tummies full eating done
Mammas resting duty done
Daddy's brewing coffee needs replete
Tents and caravans
Spick and span
Because all the family
Lent a hand
All in the spirit of Fiesta
Many lazing in sunny siesta
The Mediterranean sparkling and blue
With jumping children in brightest hue
All was wonderful, all was fun
The holiday in Spain had just begun
School books forgotten left behind
As were dreary jobs in the city grime
Now they were happy, now they were free
To camp just anywhere they wanted to be
This was the longed for Spanish sun
And the families holidays had just begun
Rich and poor side by side
Democracy, equality their guide
Huge caravans tiny tents
Tiny Volkswagons and shiny Mercedes Benz

Happy sunshine all content
All but with a single bent
Happiness with sun, sand and sea
A spacious campsite full to capacity
In San Carlos de la Rapita almond tree shaded
The sun shone bright, strong unfaded
900 souls who love the sun
In a campsite along which the road did run
The coast road from Barcelona
Running down to Tarragona
Winding tortuously hugging the coast
An ancient road of beauteous boast
Its modern twin paralleled in land
Dual carriage with toll gates manned
In San Carlos de la Rapita almond tree shaded
The sun shone brightly strong and unfaded
Here in the site of Los Alfroques
July 11th It was a Tuesday
Suddenly the sun was shaded
A huge white cloud its rays had faded
Sudden cold and icy stream
Where seconds before the heat had been
Then instantaneous as the cold appeared
A blasting furnace the air it seared
Bodies thrown, bodies burned
'Til bodies features undiscerned
Skin ripped asunder, flesh raw
Suffocated choking, breath no more
Loud bangs everywhere deafening ears
Shouting crying everywhere tears
Gas containers blasting all
All running or dying ignoring call

Screaming aflame pain unbearable
Death's kindly balm to those incurable
Human torches racing out to sea
There to extinguish before fatality
Skin ripped asunder features marred
Watches, rings melted on the peeling and the scarred
Plastic melting to drip and run
Cars twisted wreckage exploded gun
Some dead some dying some agonized in pain
Some still alight and praying for rain
Devastating black from propylene
As massive a fireball as ever seen
A mini Hiroshima as innocents felled
Machine gun bangs each second spelled
121 killed from the tanker leakage
As it passed the site to give sudden ravage
Within seconds a holocaust of flames
And soon unidentifiable bodies with no names
Germans Belgians Britons and French
Caught in 400 yards of hell and stench
Poor unhappy screaming burnt
Close to death they quickly learnt
Survivors skinned 80%
A few more hours of life to be lent
When carried off from the smoldering site
A miserable future denied of their sight
200 thus with skin peeled raw
With 43 failing to see life more
150 scarred most dreadfully hideous
Many more fading even with doctors vigorous
Children orphaned dead and scarred
This beautiful holiday totally marred

Whole families gone n'er to see more
God bless their souls they cling to Thy core
We also note had the toll road been trailed
These souls would be here their coffins unnailed
These souls were lost for but £7 cost
Had the tanker taken a different route
The sun would have shone without a doubt
No names for the dead 121
Only identification for 9 Spanniards
Whose lives were done
The others laid along a tree lined path
With a stone and a number chalked on their lathe
In Tortosa cemetery they get no rest
For who they are is anyone's guess
No nationalities no names
Anxious peering relatives , no gains
Doctors and nurses gloved hands and masks
Withdrew blood from each body aghast
Numbered and tagged with phials of glass
For to determine each blood group and class
The team came to a tiny chest
'Twas the size of an infant of 5 years or less
In the sweltering heat they continued their chore
Upon these sad souls who'd walk no more
From Germany France and Belgium too
Come forensic experts identity to prove
A hopeless task but must be tried
On the unidentifiable that hope defied
Dentition charts and scars and others
All clues to whose mother or brother
Unmelted watches and inscribed rings
And any tiny personal thing

The Bishop of Tortosa blesses and lays to rest
These poor unfortunates of scientific bequest
Scientists from England to observe and learn
If avoidance for the future they could discern
For those tankers of deathly potential
Charge past on our roads
Is daytime travel essential?
The lorry checks are once a year
So, well founded is our astonished fear
No international rules for the factories to follow
So customers only in their own ideas to wallow
Pruning metal thickness if the cost is too great
More cash profit and more money share to fete

But this must never be repeated
Legislation safe must be completed
Or death is the gas tankers terrific threat
And we do the annihilated mourn and fret
European children sprightly in the sun
The holidays had just begun

BMB-M

CLEMMIE CHURCHILL! THAT PAINTING!

Poor Clemmie how your heart did ache
When you did realize their mistake
It was your elderly, beloved's birthday treat
He who had saved us all, his enormous feat
All expectant the great man's image to unveil
To give him and us all pleasure, not to fail
But shock horror! What a stance!
We all knew it was wrong at the first glance
He, Clemmie and we all felt him mocked
Not proudly portrayed
Somehow the artists judgement
Was seriously decayed
The artists work of infinite skill
But skill's not enough without sensitive will
This painting should have been most kind
With best points underlined
For this was our hero, this Europe's saviour strong
An elderly statesmanlike image
To please the throng
His great humour and wit be accentuated
Strength from within which our great victory created
Poor unhappy instrument thou
Artist offending our sacred cow
A man who'd viewed our situation
Courageous alone in wise oration
Winston Churchill hero of the world

Who the flag of victory against cruel Hitler did unfurl
Successfully commanding our future care
Victory wrought within breadth of a tiny hair
Then later Winston suffered cruel rejection
From ungrateful Britain in the election
Poor, dear, brave, Clemmie Churchill thou
For burning the offence to our sacred cow
England applauds destruction of any offence
To this wonderful hero
For whom we have pride immense.

BMB-M

GOOD AND EVIL

Peace and wonder
Cleft asunder
By the roots of evil slain
Gathered fragments to rebuild
Fragile treasures to regain
Constant war of good and evil
Latter search in places good
The greater the source of Godliness
The closer the devil stood

BMB-M

THE LORD'S PRAYER

Infant child of maybe five
Brought the prayers in church alive
The church most sudden with innocence filled
As piping words of the Lord's Prayer spilled
In sweet sincerity profound
The tiny heart beat tender bound
And all the hearts in church did melt
As surely the Holy Spirit knelt
And warmly wrapped this tiny form
From whom the Holy words were borne

BMB-M

THE BERLIN WALL

For 15 years the wall
Has barred, has jarred, has marred
Travel banned from East to West
Shot if in escape invest
Round W.Berlin for 99 miles
15 years ago there were no smiles
As the 15feet wall rose to its height
And split their city overnight
Stacks of concrete daubed with graffiti
So no one could look and no one could see
Topped with smooth pipes to loosen the grip
So the brave or foolhardy to their agony slip
East for many metres booby traps devised
Each would be escapee would be incised
And if this does not cause the spill
Bullets from the East Tower Soviet marksmen will
The River Spree does partly form the barrier from East to West
Sadly many have found in here their final courageous rest
But many also make the terror swim to bank beyond and free
6000 annually do this feat see
At first from West are heard great cheers
But later unemployment drives their fears
But saddest of all the tales to tell
Slipped into the Spree and off into the swell
Is a little child of five
Who but for the wall would be alive
He did in May 1975
Fall in the river Spree

And did not survive
The Grepos from the East they did prevent
Firemen from the West effect the rescue bent
Poor parents of the screaming mite
Screamed desperate as he lost the fight
Oh God that such a thing could be so cruel
Prevent a sweet child's safety through guns fuel
Communist and capitalist in deadly conflict set
When is men's freedom ever to be met
When will they only sit at table there to talk.
In civilised peace and sensitivity to walk.

BMB-M

LOVELY SMELLS 1972

In the morning I leaves to the smell of burnt toast
Evenings I returns to the smells of burnt tatties
They're wonderful cooks these five girls of mine
I'll never get fat so that's just fine!

BMB-M

THE ADMIRAL'S ROOM
Southwold

It was chaos let loose in Southwold
At midnight by the sea
After Carmen at Snape and weary
We finally had the key
'Twas a night at our favourite hotel
A pressie by family given
For Daddy's 70th Birthday
A tiny bit of heaven
But not the garden room, as was expected
But just as good, the Admiral's room
"You'll like it" Tom projected
Lovely smoked salmon sandwiches
He'd made so nicely on the tray
We climbed to sight from telescope
Surveying sumptuous room array
The bathroom vast, amazing
Beckoned luxury watery joy
Clearly to the nautical
The scope too a fun new toy
TV, no sky, a fix on BBC2
But truly a rarefied pleasure
To be enjoyed by only the few
Clearly newly refurbished
With finest décor
With a 7 foot Queen's bed
With a stretch I'd adore

We were peaceful relaxing
This was much to our taste
But suddenly, rudely shattered
As we moved on with great haste
A knock and nice Tommy
Appeared again at the door
Much disturbed and apologetic
There'd been a basic flaw
The message had not been delivered
He'd not expected the Bridal pair
Just married in Yoxford in Church
Expecting the Admiral's flair
For their honeymoon here in Southwold
Hoping for sea and for sun
And booked for finest hotel
Of any there ever come
But when the pair had not on time arrived
Tommy had our ultimate comfort contrived
But now it seemed it was not to be
For honeymooners we'd surely concede
So with sandwich in hand
And in middle of munch
Out on the landing arrived with a crunch
In Nelson's bicentenary it struck us a laugh
To sit munch on the cannons
In hysterics by half
But the adjoining room frosty lady
Was definitely not amused
Tired weary exhausted
Cross and confused
No! she'd not allow gyrations more
Not even for honeymooners

Passing her door
Tommy raced up and down
Like a cat on hot bricks
Red faced and hair flapping
As he portered our bits
Then down to reception
Waited sweet loving pair
She divine in white dress
With flowers in her hair
He so crisply smart
Full regalia in tails
He did'nt much care if they slept on hay bales
After such a wondrous day of bliss
It mattered little where night's nuptial kiss
But certainly a roof they must provide
To complete perfect day
For him and his bride
Relieved that we'd not resisted
For trouble might brew
They smiled and were happy
At Admiral's luxury for two
Tommy raced us outside miles
To an Oz -like motel
To a block round the garden
As midnight befell
Flapping, rushing to room 38
No naughty Irish joke
Just an awful mistake
We were concerned the anxiety
Would now Tommy harm
But no time for an aspirin
To keep his heart calm

After major disturbance
A night undefiled
We both slept soundly
And awoke and both smiled
To a delicious breakfast
In dining room in pleasing time
Service superb in this hotel so fine
We're just pleased it worked out and pleased it was us
And not the frosty lady who'd have made such a fuss
And lets hope their marriage is as happy as ours
Starting off in their Admirals room
Their wedding and flowers.

BMB-M

AUTUMN 1993

Golden Glimpse of sun remaining
Through the woodland shafting craning
Golden flutter leaves a falling
Pheasant sound as mate is calling
Carpet red and amber gold
Fallen branches soft enfold
Dewy soft the grass a sprinkle
Blackbird flies out from the dingle
All is peaceful winter wait
Clinging leaves await their fate
Still and tranquil poised the woodland
Quiet serene in tranquil poise
Soft gentle breeze, warm, and no noise

BMB-M

THE FAMILY 1994

The family is a fountain of love and friendship
A healing balm to all within its bounds
Each giving and taking replenishment
Each experiencing its ups and its downs
Its paths of approach may vary
And often thistles found
Especially sore for tender feet
If arrogance and selfishness are around
Or if lifestyle a frown receives
Greater thorns will therein grieve
Before best healing balm is taken
Selfishness must be forsaken
From its embrace a warmth emerges
From its hugs a sweetness flows
Immense benefits with club restrictions
Every member surely knows
If restrictions recognize
Prevents the cracks and compromise
With unquestioning love
Loves each, loves all
Succouring temperature
Does not fall
To wallow in the shallows
Or swim in centre warm
Gives solace from the big hard world
And happiness finds dawn
The perfect situation
To give more than one gets

And in return gets infinite more
Than anyone directs

BMB-M

HARD MONEY MAN

Flutter flutter jack boot jerry
Off to catch the foreign ferry
Spit on gentler things that matter
Money here makes all the clatter
Family love squashed 'neath the heel
Granite hearts do stink of steel
Saddened hearts are coined as ranting
Children cluster- little banting
Try to fill the loving gap
With animals and dogs that yap
Flutter jack boot jerry
Off to catch the foreign ferry

BMB-M

MAN OF STRAW

Blustering buffoon egotistical man of straw
Why do you open then slam the door
To be a man of your word is a beacon bright
Never lack courage or shut out the light
Make no promises you cannot keep
Stretch not your legs where you cannot leap
For a man of God is sure and strong
His word is his bond and his kindness long.

BMB-M

BEAUTIFUL COUNTRY WEDDING

The lark is high
The cuckoo sound
Nestlings peep from hedgerows all around
All notes exquisite in beauty compete
From yonder hill and valley deep
Thrushes, blackbirds and warblers sing
Divine orchestral harmony bring
Lush meadows of daisies nigh
Reach to the sun in cloudless sky
Trees leafy tall and strong
Gives shade where blending hearts belong
Lambs , and cattle graze and play
Jumping for joy on this special day
Butterflies of colourful hue
As the sun doth surely dry the dew
All expressing God's own hand
In this beauteous wonderland
Where pledged the gentle lovers vow
Their goodness to the other now
Dans le jardin d'amour
Il n'ya pas de secrets entre nous
Have a marriage sweet and long
Hold hands and dance in sweet embrace
Love growing with Blessings of Heavenly Grace.

BMB-M

WIDE SMILES

Never mind the thunder
The sun will drive right through
The arching of the rainbow
Will cast its rays on you
Never mind their grizzles
Another day will dawn
Tomorrow they'll have forgotten
The things that make you yawn
But try and put your life right
And give them great big smiles
For that will warm and heal the heart
And goodness shine for miles

BMB-M

A TOUGH CHRISTMAS TIME ENCOUNTER
Banish the tough paired police traffic zealots-
Bring back our dear old Mr Plod?

In the long dark days of December
As frost bites harder than we remember
Not all are aware of God impending
Sending infant son with joy unending
For hell is thick upon the ground
With insensitivity all around
Where once stood kindly Mr Plod
Now paired toughies hit the sod
Intimidating vulnerable women lone
As rush drop child to school from home
Instead of caution kind and only pump the softer tyre
And on her way to warm cold fingers by the fire
Take 60pounds three points cruel Christmas present tend
As tearful hardworked Mum the Jesus story lend
To aggressive pair - army of unnecessary despair
As pick off easy female option there
Maybe aggressive men too much to pick from fold
Analysis may prove lone females plucked more oft from cold
Perhaps on camera interview all women should be hailed
Prevent unseen abuse, of sorts, from over zealous males
No woman should be made to cry
For an innocent ignorance of untroubling tyre
These paired toughies ideal for drugs and terrorists
Fare not well for general public health we do insist

They didn't even carry an inflating pump
To right that which their cruel campaign now trump
More specialism kindle now within the force
PCs are not all things to all folk, without remorse,
Go easy on the ladies plods of now come days
A zealous approach will bring you minimal praise
Happy Christmas!

B.M.B-M 12.12.08

OUR ADORABLE PETS

Pussy kitty nuzzle and purr
I gently stroke your thick warm furr
Blackie Tabby weave and enhance
Our busy lives as time advance
Australia, Guernsey Wales and England
Over fleeting decades five
Three sets of Blackie and Tabby
All donated loved and thrive
Golden Labs. and gold Retrievers
Jason, Julius Suzie one and two
Won our hearts waggling and woofling
Enchanting always our whole lives through
Dinah, Pinny and Nolly, nags in Oz
Arabella and Roxie
And Marti in England of course
All thro' our lives to purr, neigh, waggle
Giving love, affection
As through life we straggle
Sarah Charlotte Rebecca Emma
Our sweet daughters four
In these found solace and love
And friendship adore
As winters and summers of life
Ripple by at great speed
These wonderful family creatures
Relax and fulfill a great need

BMB-M

OUR POND

Is it not a reach of river
With rushes by the bank
Has it not a creek off South
Where moorhen chicks
Climb warm moss plank
Where willows weep o'er waters deep
And tadpoles weave, then still in sleep
Honeysuckle and bright dogrose
Waft gently in the breeze
As dinghy floats across this space with lazy summer ease
Dragonflies in bright blue hue aloft with hither thither
Ancient territorial keep whilst gently play the zither
A quiet pool of wonder, golden flowers surround
A pool of peace where thoughts freeflow
From trivial to deep profound

BMB-M 2005

YOBS

Poor parents can no longer spank
No curbs on naughty kids to bank
So a time honoured parenting "must"
No longer to parents entrust
Less dietary essentials omega sixes and threes
As fish food expensive is outfished from our seas
Violence extensive and yobs numerous as fleas
Trash food stuffed with colours and preservatives
Curdles their minds to craze and expletives
So what do you expect with these elect points
That with drugs and alcohol added
The prisons are overfull joints

BMB-M

A CHILD'S SECURITY AND HAPPINESS IS FOUND IN SIMPLICITY, NOT RICHES

Oh sweet progeny
As gold flakes shine
Around about in great profusion
Their tender lives crumble and weaken
In ultimate confusion
As parents grasp at glitter
Sleek and satin strewn
Drink drugs sex divorce
Shallow furrows for their seeds are hewn
Whilst cheap gold flitters through their fingers
And the child in riches dressed
Yet lack of simple care and time
Leaves child confused oppressed
For the real treasures are far from this scene
Care, time love the simple life
Is whence child's security would glean

BMB-M

MAJESTIC MOUNTAINS 1992

Majestic sentinels of night
Guarding what and whom
The sheep still softly grazing
And the motorist mute and lone
The dancing rivulets
At base of valley steep
Still running and dancing
When all else indulge in sleep
Guarding the sleeping red kite
Tired and weary of all day gliding flight
Guarding the furtive fox
As hunts by night he creeps
Guarding the tiny mammal
As frightened, hiding peeps
Guarding the sparse one every mile house
Where kindly farmer
Lives with loving spouse
Guarding tenderly 'til morning breaks
The ups and downs the rocks and lakes
Does the majestic mountain wide
With another self same by its side.

BMB-M 1984

FOXGLOVES 1992

Sprinkled through the mountain pasture
Foxgloves tapered gentle bells
Spring from nowhere jewels of June
High in mountains
Down in dells
Often hidden seen by no one
Then in massive army ranks
Sometimes solitary shy and lonely
Out of place on ox-eyed banks
When grasses lengthen hedges thicken
Trees are fully leafed and strong
Lambs are frisky now full grazing
Playmates jumping all day long
Birdsong peeling from the hedges
Frantic stress to feed the young
Foxgloves peel their bells in unison
Blending sweet with bird note sung
Gently sway with summer's soft winds
Curving at their finer ends
Their sturdy bed in lushest leaves
Furry plenteous largest tends
From which the purple beauty lengthens
Soft in central forest green
Warmth for central height style colour
Energy exquisite growth to glean

BMB-M 1983

WEEPING WILLOW AND SPRING

Dip your branches willow graceful

Palest green in springtime sun
Neighbours sloe forsythias almond
Balm now winters gone and done
Nodding swaying golden daffodils
Singing colours as wind dew spills
Sprinkled hedgerows mark the fields
As delicate shoots the furrows gild
Winter lacey stately stand
Trees with foliage soon to hand
Grateful for the ample storm
That spurs the growth
To new shoots born
Welcome spring today is here
Fulfilling season's tender care

BMB-M 1984

APRIL

April snow flakes flutter see
To instant melt in field and tree
Soon to vanish, welcome sun
Tiny seedlings confused begun
Minute feathery green protrude
Determination there imbued
Hedgerow field and garden scene
Green where erstwhile brown has been
Everyday some millimeters more
As shape the leaves and mount the score
Blossom too in bright array
Profusely welcome each spring day
Upward lives and nature breathes
Soon to turn the green to sheaves
Golden corn in golden twine
When spring to summer autumn find
But now it is the infant green
That clothe the earth
And lush the scene
Storm does alternate with sun
As nature's regeneration come

BMB-M 1983

WELSH CASTLES

I've dreamed to rebuild the castles
From the ruins in the hills
And renact the history
On the spot with actors skills
To shape and place their stones
With a mason's care and strength
Historians and architects
Exact the height and length
To draw in from the cities
Unemployed with TV bore
And set up camps like Baden –Powell
Wigwams in green hills to soar
Castle walls and turrets spring
Mid song and spirits high
As sunsets once more heralds
Silhouettes against the sky
Dancing fingers coloured tapestries
Idleness is scorned
Mid happy laughing voices
Of those who work from dawn
And soon this pile of misery
Mid work and fun restored
Therein to nurse a haven
Of roof, crafts, skills and more
To raise the joy of tourists
And give Welsh land delight
And further reemploy our youth
These castles of great might

And to castle chasing tourists
The drawbridge o'er the moat
With welcome in the precincts
Or a punting in the boat
Great workforce will the castles draw
And find delighted locals evermore

BMB-M 1985

A TRIBUTE TO GRANDPA

He went as he lived
With a quiet reassuring strength
The funeral quiet and simple
And of no great length
Family and close friends
And a carpet of flowers
And an abundance of love
There was a husband, father, friend
Who disliked frills but cared no end
A family doctor of tremendous skill
Who was kind and gentle
When tending the ill
A kindly Grandpa to six
For whom he had
A fund of fun tricks
He will have looked down
At his funeral with great affection
Its simplicity he'd have approved
As were it his own selection
He will have proudly watched Sue
Who fought back her tears
They were lovingly devoted for 49 years
May his spirit   her strength support
To lighten the sadness
The fears to thwart
His sons Geoff, Rob and Giles
With the love they bear
Joined all with fondest memories

*And infinite care
May he help in Heaven
As he helped on earth
Godbless Grandpa's Rebirth*

BMB-M

GET UP AND SHAKE UP

Get up and shake up
And climb that ladder of success
Rung by rung with early rise
Work with discipline
Yourself surprise
Receptive to instructions
Keep health on top of form
Humility your watchword
To avoid a storm
Get up and shake up
Horrah the job is done

BMB-M

FAITH

Let faith fill my spirit
My outlook filled with hope
Let me understand others
More than being understood
Let kindness my heart fill
My countenance strong and still
Smiling my countenance
Confidence at will
Let laughter give to others
And fun life's warmth impart
To truly radiate
With God's help
A wonderfully warm heart.

BMB-M

PROVIDENCE 2003

Life seems a tease we often find
Opportunities elude and fade unkind
But remember flowers that hide behind the leaf
Are also ready to bloom and perfume breath
Arrive flowers chance for one to grasp
Providence shines out at last
Providence to turn about
When circumstance turns inside out
Grasp and sing and hold its hand
Its always there to help you land
The things one's heart does utmost yearn
Providence may assist and fortunes turn

BMB-M

BABY BLUE TITS 2003

Golden balls of sunlight
Upon the branch so strong
In a flutter squeak together
Soon grown and flown and gone
Grasp time and hold it still
Like mercury it has its will
Make good those every moments
Flitting like the speedy bird
Away upon the wing
Make sure your moments
Tell and ring and sing.

BMB-M

WORLD MOTHERS STOP THIS CRAZY NUCLEAR BOMB RACE

(East & West) 1980

Russian Mothers
Your air is our air
Blown by the cold east wind
Nurturing cells of infinite skill
By which we breed our kith and kin
Our men they are misguided
And seek contaminate this air
'Neath guise of our protection
With their masculine warrior flair
We love your babes as t'were our babes
Sweet infants not to blame
For multiple killing missiles
Are the work of the insane
Come let us bridge our friendship
Shut out this phoney war
And let our babes now mingle
With their toys upon the floor
Let mothers tie the bow of peace
And heal the cruel wounds
Of yours and ours in battle
As they nurse their fractured bones
We each one make a Russian friend
And each to this a kindness send
We'll hurt not a hair of your cosy home

And your babes in safety keep
We'll never ravage their cosy sleep
If you die we die
And nought to save our babes
No grassy feed for our cattle
With nuclear dust ingredients of battle
We'll each make our men dissemble
These monsters they have wrought
And rid the world this menace
Which terror hopelessness hath taught
We'll n'er their beds keep warm
And their replicas not bear
Until the nuclear scourge
Has been cleared e'en from our air
Our babes will all join hands
We'll sing a song of peace
Thereafter play our part in politics
And war from thence will cease
Come eastern mothers join the west
For this plan for our world is surely the best

BMB-M

SUMMER 1987
Wales

Walk along the narrow country lane in summer
Stretch out your arms to bright array
On both sides to touch the flowers
For here is where the rabbits play
Leaping from their bowers
Here wave the stately foxgloves
Shake and ring their bells
The campion, forget me nots
With colour splash the hills
Tall grow green grasses
Butterflies catch the sun
As summer seems to race so fast
No sooner come than gone
Breath sweetly in the perfumes
Examine close the flowers
For they are but a short while here
To brighten up our hours
A touch God's joy from Heaven
That must never miss your gaze
And spare a peep o'er yonder hill
Where cows do chew and laze

BMB-M

THE EXQUISITE ROSE - A TENDER HEART

There is no greater gift from God
Than a sweet and tender heart
Steeped in spring-like magic
Of all that can impart
Sparkling with transparent kindness
And actions full of wholesome couth
Bear all responsibility and kind hearted truth
With infinite cheerfulness
A helping hand to always share
Lightening other's sorrows
Make them easier to bear
Therefore sweet child infant
Of love and quiet repose
God give you now a tender heart
In your spirit's garden
Grows the exquisite rose

BMB-M

WEDDING SONG
Dawn and Eric 2004

Life is wonderful
Life is sweet
Dawn and Eric are married
To make life complete
The birds sing
And sunshine sparkles
And blooming flowers
Their pathway sprinkles
And life is full of joy, hope love
And Blessings warm
From God above
Dawn's beauty exquisite in white
Eric enthralled
The future bright
Guests smiling
Confetti and fun
Lets celebrate this marriage just begun
We wish a loving ,long life, sweet
With babes to make their lives complete
Love, patience, fun and constant laughter
Peace, health, joy for ever after

BMB-M

BLUEBELLS

2002

The air was sweet with new mown grass
Soft with dew not long to last
Warming fingers of bright sunlight
Filled with migrating birds so fast
The merest movement of the softest breeze
Nodding the full bloomed bluebells
With exquisite ease
Sturdy strong in beauty
With cowslips and primroses gold
Now that spring has petals
And lambs leap o'er daffodil fold
We breath the ecstasy of regeneration found
In wonderful springtime all around

B.M.B-M.

9/11 SAVAGING OF NEW YORK

9/11/01
150 immense stories high
The twin Towers were demolished
So cruel from the sky
By rogue pilots, innocents on board loaded
Flew directly into buildings
Which immediate exploded
The disbelieving world in horror stood
As precious lives were drenched in blood
Thousands previous at work desks smiled
Before the impact planes defiled
From 80 nations around the world
½ mast flags in misery unfurled
Chaos reigned and fury blast
Frail humans lost their spirits grasp
Sunshine eclipsed by deadly smoke
Courage and kindness o'er took these folk
As patient lines took stairs step by step
Feeling in darkness as injured fret
Helping carrying slowly care
Aware, terrified desperate, full of fear
And sudden floors by the masses collapse
Thousands of lives lost with this new crash
Widows, widowers orphans in moments made
As families loved ones breathing fade
Some finished by leap from windows in terror
Falling snowflakes to despairing onlookers horror
So desperate to help yet to do so was death

But brave firefighters died leaving families bereft
Never of God these evil suicide missions
Creating misery and death only Satan's vision
To kill the flowers of 80 nations
Is surely no less than a serious invasion
Ruin and tragedy met innocent lives
The bell tolls for 3000 in those deadly dives
Godbless these and their families left
And erase from our world
The devil's evil cleft

BMB-M

GOD IN THE GARDEN AT PLAS PADARN

In the still of monastic procession
Our garden prides its peace
As plain song haunts the willows
Mercy pervades and seeps
Ecclesiastical grace wraps the roses
Witchhazel blooms on Christmas Day
Hydrangeas full rusty autumn blooms
Nodding monks avoid worldly fray
The wind through the roses whispers prayers
Sometimes rises to praise at full height
The glorious sound of men's voices
Declaring God's wonderful might
The birds too feel sacred here hallows
Adoring and joyous in song
Productive and caring their feathered mites
In flight before cold winter long
Stand still for a moment and savour
Of goodness this garden divine
As its memories of monks in procession
8 centuries past, cloistered fine

BMB-M

MOTHER CHRISTMAS GIVES JOY TO THE LONELY ELDERLY AND NEEDY

In ancient Aberystwyth
Born on monastic site
Where bells ring in granite Churches
Where mountains and seas delight
A charity for the goodly
To give to those with less
A traditional meal on this Holy day
And with their kindness Bless
The giants of catering industry
Bend their gentle hands
To present this festive gift
In cities thro' out our land
Salvation Army their banners nigh
Gather the needy, no praise too high
Social services, Samaritans and Age Concern
Comb the community
Their needs to learn
But at individual level true Mother Christmas lay
As shrieks of laughter wrap happy Christmas Day
The family bears a plate of their precious Christmas meal
Children's radiant faces show their sweetly joyous zeal
There to smile at the gathering
With food to an elderly person given
Is this not truly a goodly touch of Heaven
Smiles all round warmth imparted

The Christchild is all about love
And warm hearted.
Nothing simpler could be extolled
No cost encountered, God's gift behold

BMB-M

RAMBLA NOVA TARRAGONA

Spain
Happy, happy, happy place
The Rambla Nova's happy face
Sauntering laughing children beside
The well fed pidgeons in and out glide
Toddlers running to set them in flight
As parents run to gather escaping mite
These infants dressed in exquisite cotton
Rueshed and smocked expense forgotten
For these are children adored beyond all
Loved and cosseted the Deity's call
No child abuse in Spain we scent
For these young are for best love meant
Teenagers clique for fun and style
Wrapped deep in converse joy and smile
Grannies gather over pram to beam
Excited by the sweet child seen
Tickle bambinos as wheeled in display
Under feathery trees, on marble this day
Pregnant ladies smartly dressed
Husband's loving arms protected Blessed
Saunter slowly so little to wait
For little joy its life to wake
Men with wives and children walk
A mile up Ramblas meet friends talk
Evening warm the sun set called
Fun and chattering its length installed
Balcony by sea, dancers on stage

Catalan piping music colours the page
Bright dresses, so perfect , the footwork so exact
Sadanas enchant the audience spellbound rapt
Sudden finish that complete
Audience rushes to find more replete
Castillas mount people higher and higher
With a small child on the top to act as the flyer
In uniform smart each team after other
If too ambitious in height
Brother falls upon brother

On Fiesta days the giants in procession
With reedy band marks out special occasion
Round the town giving festive delight
When daylight turns now into night
What a splendid show for the Ramblas Nova
To be seen in Fiesta from April to October

BMB-M

MAGGIE THE GREAT

(P.M. Lady Margaret Thatcher)

Bodacea, Joan of Arc, Elizabeth the First
And Maggie the Great
Led men of their time
As was their great fate
What greater curse could they choose to follow
As driving a stubborn donkey called ego
Is difficult and hollow
Hiding their gentleness with charm and efficiency
Made men think they were leading
But this was a fallacy
A product of our great grammar schools
Which were closed by English enemies or fools
As were those who would Barts Hospital have closed
Maggie would have stopped this lunacy
On scheming bureaucrats her venom loosed
A Major fool lacked wisdom and let bad bureaucrat reign
To attack 1000 years of Barts maybe e'en for personal gain.
This touchstone of excellence of medical height
Was nearly closed outright.
Her wisdom would never such excellence maim
Her insight too incise to give conspirator fame
A grocers daughter was no other
But note, nurtured by principles each grocer must cover
Hard work diligence and detail attended
Kind to his customers to avoid the offended
Astute awareness of mice and rats

Swift eradication to keep establishment in tact
For rats and vermin in Government be
Who better to exterminate those
Than our remarkable Maggie
Evaluating all she chose
Recognition of loyalty in customers and service
Helps fill the purse and strengthen premise
Working 'til late and up at dawn
Even if tired and feeling forlorn
Those principles to keep a good shop
Instilled from birth takes her rule to the top
With courage take the troups the Fawkland War to fight
Our British territory protect with all the forces might
But woe are those who plot to topple this fine Tory
They blood let the Tories now struggling and gory
The rats had found another hole
To break the heart of this finest English maid
The conspiracy would Labour beckon and bade
Those twitching wretches will nay rest
With swords so sharp they cut the best
It wreaked and smelt corruption beast
And fair did wreck the Tory feast
A similar fate great Barts Hospital nearly take
Good health from fine food the grocers wife fed her
Great belief in her abilities her father had led her
A fine talent for work and detail aware
A fearless courage
The unions this fine lady sort and scare
With smart exterior and expert diplomatic flair
The union grip she shifted, laid bare
Our country torn apart by unions no more
Maybe this was her finest victory score

A ship shape government she efficiently plied
Ambassadress skillful foreign powers she'd guide
With her loving, adoring Dennis by her side
Mountainous paperwork
Speed read into night and understood
This formidable intellect this strain withstood
Let not lesser lights diminish her glow
For such as she you'll seldom know
The test of time will mark her fame
Maggie the Great our greatest dame

BMB-M

SYCAMORE AUTUMN SCENE

Stately vast against the sky
Sycamore stretches its branches high
Sturdy, bold, courageous strong
As clouds amongst its branches throng
Roots astraddle in the stubble
Golden harvest gathered in
Geese are pecking at the grain
Far beyond tho' eyes do strain
Autumn winds now snatch the leaves
Thrusting, flattering tearing thieves
Gold confetti on the wing
The crisp north westerly wind to bring
Clouds impending soon to drench
As golden wonder from sycamore wrench
Saddened tree stands naked shorn
The savage winds undress forlorn
Soon unclothed and shivering stand
As ploughman turns the ancient land
As through the centuries till the soil
By sweat of brow his kind arms toil
Strong and caring of his flock
The land in balance with his stock
This tree has countless seasons seen
As land prepared and corn is gleaned
And knows as only patient wait
Soon come springs sweet greenly gait.

BMB-M

A SURPRIZE MOTHER CHRISTMAS MEAL FOR MRS KAY ON CHRISTMAS DAY 1990

So quiet and cold this Christmas Day
Granny huddles over tray
Crumbs beneath a grimy plate
Crumbs beneath her feet she hate
Wants her extra Oxfam woolie
Too much pain to move her body
3 years back her Herbert died
He'd have helped, he'd have tried
Lonely quiet, no children near
No one to help no one to hear
Flats above around beneath
Loneliness they do bequeath
People busy, no stop and care
Enjoying themselves but her cupboard bare
Peer from window now quiet street
No shoppers with bags replete
Cold comfort, cold day
'Tis no Christmas for Mrs Kay
A knock at noon on door. A call!
"Mrs Kay I'm here to take you to the hall"
She nodded off she did not hear
She preferred to sleep than lonely bear
"Mrs Kay Mrs Kay answer please!
"Yes I'm coming
I'll find the keys"

Arthritic joints to door so slow
"I'm coming " she murmured "I'm coming now"
Painful release of bolts and padlock turned
Thro' chained crack she peer, fear burned
In the lonely eyes of Mrs Kay
High rise fear she knew each day
But kindness thro' the crack she saw
As she opened the chain on the creaking door
Kindness shone in this stranger dear
Dispelling her fright and wiping a tear
For Mrs Smith slow-dressed these bones arthritic bound
With clothes and smartening 'til a smile she found
We're off for a meal for Christmas Day
Merry Christmas Mrs Kay
The Church hall was all festive bright
Burning with people and colour and light
Christmas carols and a happy sound
Old folks at the table all around
What a surprise for Mrs Kay
She'd quite forgotten treats of Christmas day
Christian kindness fun and joy was there
Release from loneliness and despair
Straightway a family plate they bear
Piled high with turkey and Christmas fare
The children delighted also smiling and smart

To old Mrs Kay they warmed her heart
She thanked their kindness and Christmas joys
And waved to the exit those sweet girls and boys
The delicious meal so tasty hot
Loneliness at this party quite forgot
Crackers pudding laughter and fun

A hall of joy as bright as the sun
For the elderly and lonely the town truly cared
And their Christmas feasts so generously shared
A happy day so freely given
A tiny tiny touch of Heaven
To the flat Mrs Kay returned
Full of gratitude her dear old heart burned
Herbert would have loved that happy day
She thought as her head on her pillow lay
People delivering a feast laden Christmas meal plates
Their hearts to warm their spirits elate
To give lonely needy and elderly such a wonderful party
Seldom she'd seen the town so loving and hearty
Giving company, no cost and smiley fun party
A little touch of "Jesus-in-manger-lay"
Heavenly Heaven on Christmas Day

BMB-M

JUBILEE PROJECT
25 years of Queen Elizabeth 2
Guernsey-1977

If its youth involvement you want to see
In this celebrated year of the Jubilee
We suggest to music the community turns
For an youth orchestra this island yearns
Youngsters who are bored and turn to crime
Give 'em a trumpet from your donated dime
Let 'em blow off that energy excess
And blast out music- well more or less
Concentration increased 200%
And healthy exhaustion to a great extent
Get something of which we'll all be proud
Let 'em play both long and loud
Entertain the elderly and those depressed
With their music trained to the very best
Let them travel to see lands new
International language is the musical cue
Let them camp and feel pure air fresh
And fill it with music, vigour and zest
Come Guernsey back with political financial leaven
And establish a youth orchestra in 1977

BMB-M

BETTY'S FUEL

Conflict is her fuel of life
On offence and mischief thrive
And yet inside this complex soul
A more enduring is alive
Is she supersensitive
Of miniscule thin skin
Whose aim in life to throw those spears
That pain so much within
Perhaps to childhood days it dates
When sibling baby arrived
And poor little Betty was forgot
In drama of babe to survive
But nearly ninety years have flown
Since something wounded that child
Who maybe handled a little differently
Would now be kind and mild
And save others so much suffering
And wounds throughout the years
What is the psychology
As she hurls her unkind spears
So quick to fault
And slow to praise
Throughout her long ½ million days
But yet I think another cause has set her in her ways
She had no babes, no child to love
Regret it all her days
And now that she and darling man
They've toiled now 9 decades

They have no loving grown up kids
Their hours to warm and aid
No letters come, no visits
From kith and kin so made
Altho' so good to each other
Children would fear now fade
When the other departed for ever
There'd be someone near and dear
So we guess that's the cause of the frost
That her companions have to bear
But better to find that other source of love
The One who adores us from above.
To kneel on the hassock
And sing with the heart
Find sooth and solace with God
With the love that impart.

BMB-M 1988

JULIUS OUR WONDERFUL GOLDEN RETRIEVER

Strength, joy, love within this gem
Bounds off on family walks
In and out the rabbit holes
As scents and leads he stalks
Racing here and racing there
This golden fluff of speed
Then rushes back to master's side
As whistle heard he heed
Then stretch the length of golden beach
And splashing in the shallows
This wooflie whirlwind fleet-foot-wow
Fountain-shakes, a-scatter
At home he snuggles closer
Each person sweetly there to nudge
A loving vac of this and that
And chocolate and fudge
Those sweetest soft brown pleading eyes
Just melt our good intent
And even if he's had too much
We really do relent
If all people had the heart
Of this dear dog in our sad world
There'd be no wars or terrorists
But a mighty peace-flag there unfurled

BMB-M

LAST DAY OF FINALS AT OXFORD

Bowler hatted bulldogs
Students revelry around
To greet the final papers
Beaten to the ground
Pale and tired and overwrought
Forgotten all were ever taught
They struggle to the gate
The end of the beastly finals
Everyone's pet hate
Revelers thrust them flowers
And wave and shout and hug
Balloons and champagne bursting
O'er poor emerging mug
Whose face explodes with laughter
At the pranks of loving friends
Flushed capillaries pallor flees
Affection makes amends
For unmitigated purgatory
2 papers every day
In search of a degree
A glimmer reaches may
In any case unruly throng
Pushes shouts and surges
As each poor exhausted victim
From exam. hall now emerges
And then there's little Emma
Whose friends had flown last year
Only poor old Mum out there

To give that final cheer
She's out there with the flowers
Balloons she has in double
Sun gleam o'er ancient cobbles
To comfort waif in trouble
The smiles are really hard to coax
Exhausted thin and pale
Examinitis worn and fraught
Hair long and figure frail
Blinks as she sees the massive throng
Unruly loud and fun
But not for her the milling crowd
Its only her old Mum
Smiling big encouragement
Come on! Life's just begun!
The papers grueling all behind
And sunshine in the sky
Lets shake off care and start to live
And keep those spirits high
A bonfire make of all those notes
The candle late forget
Oxford finals are history
No further slave and fret
Go phone the gang and tell them
You too have seen the last
Of the nasty finals papers
And can now break fun's long fast

BMB-M

MR MAJOR'S MAJOR DISASTER

(ST BARTHOLOMEWS HOSPITAL LONDON
Founded 1123 A.D.)

Mr Major Mr Major what a major disaster
Your inaction was inadequate
Undesirable of master
Responsibility defied
The people's ownership denied
Did you not suspect skullduggery abound
We all did, why was't not found
Were you not suspicious
Developers tentacles malicious
Sought new hospital to build
Purse with NHS gold get filled
Fill cash vacuum to be meeting

First they tried in London South
Before being booted out
You as head of Governement
These plotters should have sought
The very best in Britain
Your protection sure you ought
But sad those tricks
You failed to fix
And goodness was attacked
It surely was not Barts
But you they should have sacked!

BMB-M

MY WONDERFUL HUSBAND

My darling you're my treasure
A friend valuable beyond world's measure
The dear love of my life
I am your loving wife
Holding hands and sharing all
For nearly fifty years our call
Father Mother sister brother
Each has been towards the other
Sharing food upon the table
Sheltering 4 darling offspring
As much as able
Laughter joy and stress and care
Fun with friends, sad, some not there
Romance and peaceful pass the nights
As gently flies the marriage flight
Maybe far away in time
Maybe soon we're not to know
Our spirits, hand-in-hand together fly
From life's various paths to float on high
You are mine and I am yours
To happiness the very source
With our God us on to guide
Let the sunshine warmly shine
Stay fit and well and happy be
With our loving family and
Divinely Rob&JB

BMB-M

EXQUISITE SUNSET

Oh gentlest night approaching fast
Divinely sunset can't long last
Brilliant flaming orange ball
Poised quiet serene 'er night shall fall
Milky quietly heaving sea
Of palest lavender and palest green
Stippled from shore to farthest line
This duet in colour exquisite fine
A boat, where breaks a line of white
Tiny throbbing before the night
Caught luminous orange shaft
To lighten up this small boat craft
A pool so still to glass it turns
Reflection holds the ball that burns
The sky in bands of four stood still
Pale blue gave clue of summers fill
And then pale grey a band across
Repeated to horizon lost
And in between with firey ball
Was lit an orange streaking scroll
Oh beauteous sunset stay awhile
God's peace and presence here to smile

BMB-M

CHILD ABUSE

That savagery doth leave its mark
The tree is gutted and leaves the bark
Psychiatrists and parents the wound may heal
The soul restored the breach to seal
A boy's true manhood may n'er achieve
Homosexual sadness the wound to leave
Sex warped and not as God decreed
No adoring children to care and feed
A girl may promiscuous or lesbian become
Not sweet with beloved husband sun
Uncontrolled lust their petals hath torn
No fault of innocent flower there shorn
Victims of a twisted savage snake
When misdirected engenders and hate
Honour knows it not with a wrong heart
Yet maybe they similar victims of twisted dart
Would that science could rest men of their curse
If instrument of love they do not nurse
To free of detonator dark
And wake free of torment pure as lark

BMB-M

MOTHER CHRISTMAS

On Christmas Day
Lets give some fun
To the elderly and needy
With family Christmas none
As the lights upon the tree
Shine in a happy blaze
Lets light up our hearts
And our kindly meal gift raise
Kids crowd round the turkey
In their velvets and their smiles
And cheer as Daddy carves
The very best turk for miles and miles
And Mummie, oh so beautifully
The vegs does arrange
Upon this plate most special
Take it to elderly, lonely person strange
Big family smiles it looks so good
This gift of traditional Christmas food
The children clap and loudly cheer
They lift the plate so proud to bear
A small gift colourful and candle bright
And off to Church hall's gathering of joy and light
Christmas tree, trimmings and lots of happy faces
Helpers and guests streaming in from many places
Christian joy is there so amazingly evident
Here's another family their contribution lent
In microwave the plate is now receiving heat
Who's the next guest to receive this treat

To the next in line the children give their gift
And someone attends the candle the brightness lift
Pull your cracker with me, let me put on your hat
Your lovely food is here
What do you think of that
As were it there the Holy Child
Sweet children smile
The power of sweet giving magic pervades
Carols sudden start as music is made
Happy happy Christmas everyone
A happy party where there would have been none
Daddy and the children wave goodbye
And race back home
Where Mum has made the gravy
Horray their own Christmas meal time come

BMB-M

LADIES RESTORE YOUR MORALS

There was once woman called Greare
Who said girls go live life more freer
Now there are no kids
And no husbands with quids
And life is that much more drear
Nasty infections eat at the flesh
The host not quite so much of a dish
Free living and pill
Makes their lives dirtier still
Greare know happiness not wrapped up in freer

Lets get back to clean Victorian prude
Promiscuity promotes its punishment crude
Christianity would these people restore
Monogamy it really must implore
Jumping from pillar to post
Spiritually cripples the host
Girls make monogamy your personal law

For promiscuity is not Christian
A chastity ring more honourable make
Marry and be good to each other
Exclusivity civilization make.

BMB-M

THE LOVING SISTERS ALEX AND MARY

Where's your laughter
At Plas Padarn deep in Wales
Every inch vibrated
With your fun and mirth
In gales
Your gratitude eternal
Made it such joy to give
Your deep religious sincerity
Shewed how we all should live
And now its quietly silent
Where that laughter should be rife
We listen for the echos
And instead we know your strife
Stroke struck quickly sudden
And your zest for life was still
For a month the nurses slaved
Then of daylight took your fill
You'd staved off pneumonia
And with nasal tube was fed
And overturned four hourly
In this life upon the bed
North Road they fought courageous
To see this dear old lady live
For even with a twinkle
She had a lot to give
Response it flickered more each day

Sweet sister Mary sat to pray
Each morning by the bedside
Where her dear sweet sister lay
She battled up the steep steep hill
From Deva to this spot
E'en with her central vision gone
Self pity not a jot
The winds howled round about her
As each step she bravely took
To will some life in Alex
Other interests all forsook
She was herself but 89
And Alex two years younger
The tears they streamed down aging cheeks
As sister torn asunder
She sang to her some favourite hymns
That mother had them taught
She said" you had a finer voice
Dear Alex-made me fraught"
We remember at the Rectory piano
As mother sweetly sat
While all we children sang these hymns
With dog and favourite cat
Now Alex tried to sing as well
But not a sound would come
But her mouth it broadly smiled....
As she twinkled in the sun
Another bout pneumonia
Had set her back once more
But she regained her conciousness
To nod the hymns encore
We clustered round her bedside

To fan this gift of life
So much enjoyed by Alex
And salvaged from the strife
Mary's hope so cherished
For she'd lost her daughter dear
Was to keep this light in Alex
Brightening as she passed her near
The sisters drew from others strength
As when they played when young
Perhaps their parents fondly gazed
And with them sweetly hymns now sung

BMB-M

2005 BICENTENARY OF NELSON'S DEATH
A PEN SKETCH AND VERSE ON HORATIO NELSON

Born September 29 1758   Burnham Thorpe Norfolk
Died 21st October 1805 at Battle of Trafalgar aged 47 years

Parents: Rev Edmund Nelson married Catherine Suckling from
Barsham, Beccles 1749
11 children, 3 died at birth, 7 died before Horatio
William Susannah and Kitty survived after Nelson's death

He was tiny mischievous and fun
Tiny dare devil's life begun
From the rectory
In Burham Thorpe
Here was a pickle
Often caught
Daddy the rector
To Burham Church
To Matins on Sunday
This monkey to search
Escaping from the pew at two
Well loved in everybody's view
With congregation giggling
At the antics of this child
In middle of sermon
Infant fun and free and wild

As father from the pulpit spoke
Pursued down the aisle by Nelson folk
A happy carefree life with gardens, land
And ships in sail in Kings Lynn at hand
Trips to see sailors ahoy and bobbing boats
Rippling water, reflected floats
With eager children horse and trap
Picnic aboard and smart their cap
From the house kiddies all excited
Ships of strangers all delighted
Sailors fast fix mast and rigging
Whilst at work their shanties singing
This would be a treat indeed
Young Nelson for his future feed

✯✯

His mother taught her children eight
To read and write and manners make
Whilst servants 4 dealt with the chores
Make the food and scrub the floors
A happy life on Norfolk land
With nature kerbed with labourer's hand
In the tumbrels rumbling riding
In and out the sheaves a hiding
When harvest came with ripened wheat
Riding on the wagon seat
With labourers kids aboard as well
They were his pals he got on swell
Later on Victory as his crew to work
Double the worth of the city shirk
Ideal environment a dare devil make
As a child on the land
Future world would shake

He slid down stack
And on cart horses ride
Where children love to
Run, play hide
A wild free lovely country life
Learning to cope with peace and strife
But sadness came when he was nine
This poor child lost his mother fine
The greatest sadness in his earth
Around the time of Kitty's birth
His rock, his treasure, mother gone
To join the Heavenly angels throng
Then he and William to school away
Leaving father home to pray
At Norwich then to Paston later
Harsh life bare boards
He'd learn to cater
They now in North Walsham found
His energized with plenty ground
At Paston school he clever show
And lively mischievous boys to know
One evening espy some ripe ripe pears
In the walled garden just down below
But fierce Head Price Jones of these was proud
And there'd be trouble, his boys were cowed
All so terrified but Horatio said "I'll go"
Dare devil heart they had in tow
They lowered him within a sheet
To the garden down in excitements heat
And up again his haul intact
The head not seen this naughty fact
A feast was had upon the floor

Whilst someone else did watch the door
But Horatio of it ate none
Purely for the dare he had that done
Expected trouble now to brew
The Head scowled upon the few
In wrath with bribe he tapped his cane
Five guineas did he wave again
A tempting bribe indeed
For purses did those pennies need
"Who did upon my ripe pears feed?"
But silence met his just demand
Nelson gazed upon faces calm
Their loyalty to him was welcome balm
Whose pocket was more a-pressing?
Never a sound, he had their Blessing!
They'd no more split on Nelson
Even though 5 guineas much
They were band- of- brothers
Mr Jones was out of touch
Which boy he taught he never knew
Had risked his life to feed the few
Which boy emerged their hero such
Honour strong admire him much
These kids they stuck together strong
Their friendship would be good and long
✶✶

In holiday with Pa at Burnham Thorpe
Off on Ponies to ships they sought
Or to Barsham Rectory to have fun
With parents of poor lost Mum
And Susannah, Ann and Kitty too
Dear sisters of these lively two

Horatio's uncle Maurice Suckling met
Influenced Horatio a sailor set
For he a Captain of ship at sea
How much Horatio that longed to be
When he was twelve stand proud on deck
With sailor 'chief tied round his neck
"Well if at school you do not shirk
I'll take you to sea for sailor work."
✯✯

Father survived on land and tithes
He did his best his children thrive
So sad without his lovely wife
To steer his children out of strife
The children avoided the maladies of the day
Malaria, Smallpox, Diphtheria
So quick to take life away
Susannah and Kitty apprenticed to
Millinery and lace
Both married merchants
And lived in reasonable grace
But the boy Nelson went to sea at twelve
✯✯

March 1771

Nelson aboard 64 gun HMS RAISONABLE
Protected by his Captain uncle Maurice able
Whom he loved, respected and sat at table
To sea to settle Fawkland Islands ownership disaster
But when the Spanish saw the Royal Navy
They backed off sailing even faster
Then to Merchant ship in West Indies trade
Much education on navigation made

Less discipline than Royal Navy in action
But effective order aboard with satisfaction
On return from Indies West
Took to serious training to learn his best

1772
Had 9 months studying, sailing vessels small
At Chatham avoiding tidal and sandbank haul

Excited aboard HMS CARCASS a great ambition
For scientific ARCTIC EXPEDITION
Under Captain Lutwidge to the big freeze bound
Reached Spitsbergen surprised still mild they found
Chronometers by Harrison and Arnold in cold to test
So turned up north in frozen clime rest
Stuck in ice for 2 days then rose the wind
Released from jam in which ship firmly pinned
On to Fairhaven with varying fog with gales
Frightening experience up and down with sails
Scientific work and tests assigned to make complete
Crews of ships happy working in warm sunshine replete
Magnificent setting sun like jewels in the sky
To dazzle and glitter astonished eye
Incredible beauty and spouting whale
Young Nelson hunted a bear, not fail
Racehorse and Carcass ships in danger, ice full lock
Provisions hauled in small boats to hold food stock
Nelson in charge of Cutter pulled 4 miles over ice
To open sea when ships released caught up suffice
They were mighty anxious but enchanted with this place

Approach to Spitsbergen, relief and celebration saved by Grace
A fine attitude of calm in all emergencies was John Baird
His example to young Nelson would well have fared

Aboard 24 gun SEAHORSE in 1776
Captain Farmer his next mentor his uncle fix
To make way from Portsmouth to Cape Hope
Was well within their their sailing scope
Then to Madras when sails intact
For 53 days warm waters lapped
3 months Madras in port
Ten East Indies ships escort
1400 miles from Bengal to Basra under sail
Enormous journey too long at sea, stale!
At Bombay Nelson won £300 on gaming tables
If he'd lost there'd have been no fables
Sent home on Dolphin when with malaria very ill
Saved by the kindness of James Pigott with various pill
He'd been away three years at sail
To recover health soon English shores hail

Then when health restore
He must of the salt have more
With Captain Robinson on WORCESTER of 64 gun
Escorting as 4th Lieutenant to Gibraltar begun
Until suddenly crippled by a dangerous gale
But assisted by Spanish fishermen into Cadiz to sail

1777
In London City the naval books to swot

At 18 Lieutenants exam he got
He can now splice, knot, reef and sail
And knows his flag semaphor when out of hail
With 45,000 miles under sail cloth at sea
Great experience to expect seniority

On HMS LOWESTOFT aboard
To height of 2nd Lieutenant soared
2nd Lieutenant to Captain William Locker
Role was to defend trade ships against the enemy blocker
American privateers and others in Caribbean scene
Facing fierce hurricanes in mountainous seas

1778
HMS BRISTOL
Nelson's fast ascendancy up the ranks saw him promoted to
first Lieutenant from third, promoted over other heads
Admiral Parker recognized his brilliance
1778 December
NELSON'S FIRST CAPTAINCY
Aboard HMS BADGER

Gulf of Honduras to Spanish land
British settlers he now warns first hand
Spanish war approaching fast
And French flags likely to pin to masts

Nelson's mast damaged in storm
Refit required to Badger forlorn
Careening wharf at Royal Port

To clean the hull was sought
Then first prize, La Prudente caught
But this ship was allowed to sail free
His very first prize disallowed at sea
To Nelson's real dismay
He thought him rich upon this day
Alas not so!

NELSON Aboard HMS HICHINBROKE
HIS FIRST COMMAND OF A SHIP

Of Hichingbroke he took command
To West Indies where health harmed
Of 1400 on expedition 380 survive
Dysentry, yellow fever and malaria steal their life
Nelson's malaria marred his health once more
Became so ill his command did hit the core
Wrong timing might have been one reason
San Juan river maybe possible in dry season
Nelson taken to Admiral Parker's Jamaican house
Nursed, and ills with herbal remedies douse

Aboard AMITY HALL
With malaria ill did fall

On HMS Amity Hall for further care sailed home
To restore his health priority had now come
Whilst on this ship his stern command expose
Noting insubordination of the Captain close
His fury knew no bounds
As recalcitrant he hounds

And temper cross we note
And patience gone as now afloat

1780
recuperation from malaria
in Bath, England
Went to Bath to rest and recover
Several months with malaria to suffer

1781
Aboard HMS ALBERMARLE
Command
For Baltic expedition

Men raised from London for the ship then were raised
And some friends from Wells in Norfolk he'd praised
With HMS Enterprise and HMS Argot
To Elsinore in Denmark attack the foe
Ships full of timber, pitch and tallow from afar
Swedish iron, hemp and the best Stockholm tar
To build U.K. ships now under Nelson's escort safe
Avoiding Russian, Danish and Swedish hostile shake

1782
Abermarle accidentally damaged at anchor in The Downs
Needing extensive repairs causing some frowns
Then off to Quebec and a Nelson prize at last
Of Madiera wine and schooner fast
From American privateer unexpected
Sent it to Quebec with crew elected

But this voyage marred by scurvy in Albermarle crew
Undermining health and welfare in more than few
✯✯

Mary Simpson at the Garrison Ball
Captivated Nelson in love to fall
But sadly his purse her beauty did not match
She had eyes for a wealthier catch
"You are not the match for me"
She sent him forlornly back to sea
Elizabeth Andrews when to Norfolk returned
She too his marriage proposal spurned
A young officer on £150 a year
Could not in style for a lady care
So loves young dream again frustrated
Back to ships where work was catered

1783
Nelson in St Omer France for French to learn
As in 1784 to govern democratic Britain
To William Pitt elected turn
202 ships were commissioned 1784
Whilst peacetime for Nelson
Involved entertainment, expense and more

Then command aboard a 28 gun frigate
On HMS BOREAS in 1784
The following year eager West Indies to explore
Nelson falls in love again
Francis Nesbit to adore
She had a 5 year old son Josiah
A busy time combining sailings

And courting Francis much admire
With aboard 150 crew
Set sail Antigua to view
On MARCH 11<u>TH</u> 1787
<u>Nelson secured romantic heaven</u>
The King of heroism a husband happy became
Francis Nisbet of Nevis delighted wed her swain
Given away by a Prince
Who they barely saw since
Her child now had a new father fun
As playing boating and ships a new interest begun
Then the little family went to Norfolk
For country life for five long years
Reaping the apples the orchard bears
Veggies and corn did he help to grow
Watching the seasons come and go
Collecting with Josiah birds eggs from the nest
Teaching the child identify wildlife he knew best
In summer to saunter with Francis hand in hand
Sweet times and family fun
But he preferred drama at sea to peace at land
However no one offered him command of a ship
He felt rejected, frustrated
In the brine he must dip
For nautical action he brilliantly shone
Directionless on land his brilliance gone
As he waited for a ship command anew
It seemed an age for that to view
It came with the French revolution
Now Agamenmon would be the solution
So he gathered his men from Wells and around
Far better quality than those press-ganged found

Off to the sea for a much greater fee
And Nelson also took now grown Josiah
To teach the child of ships and sea
As a modest country gentleman with 5 years ashore
On half pay in Burnham Thorpe at last was no more
In 1793 evil swept the French shallows
French revolution, Louis XVI to the gallows
And his lovely Queen savaged, put to death
Turmoiled country, sorrow, misery
Throughout its length and breadth
Then on England and Holland declared war
Illconceived wretches more death to score
Troops rushed together, hurriedly assembled
England and Holland much activity resembled
Ships gunneries soldiers prepared
Nelson relished action and better fared
His Command aboard Agamemnon HMS
Helped capture Corsica nonetheless
Saw battle at Calvi but he lost his right eye
His binocular vision seriously deny
From 1796 to 97 for a period 6 months pursue
Commodore on HMS Captain
Rear Admiral of Blue
With Captain Berry mid the Cape St Vincent battle hard
Nelson bold and valiant did superiors orders disregard
But he gained victory by heroic brilliant dash and dare
The dangers which made less heroic men
Blanch and turn and scare
On HMS Captain sailed dash to divide the Spanish fleet
Sword on board San Nicholas now he and others leap
The Spaniards surrendered or faced the mighty deep
Victorious mighty acclaimed the mighty British fleet

As once again by Nelson's astuteness and valour
The deadly enemy unseat

Aboard HMS THESEUS assignment danger next
Led an 8 ship squadron attack the Spaniards vex
Merchant ships at Santa Cruz on Tenerife alarm
But sad this operation cost Nelson his right arm

Here poor Nelson was injured in the elbow on the right
His caring young stepson, Josiah, held the tourniquet tight
The cruel musket had shattered his saluting arm
Nelson saluted crew with left so as not to draw alarm
The crew his fortitude viewed with disbelief
With excruciating pain bravely bore his grief
Bore the amputation with true stoicism
This living legend of unrivalled heroism
Never again to see the like
Of Horatio Nelson so brave in fight

In 1798 Horatio Nelson was justly Knighted
England recognizing greatness was truly now delighted

Then aboard HMS VANGUARD in the battle of the Nile
Again exhibits leadership no one ever would deny
Routed out cunning French fleet hiding in Aboukir Bay
And destroyed 11 ships of the French naval line that day
The greater fleet was shattered as the rest from battle fled
Nelson once more acclaimed a hero with glory on his head
Even more promotion genius granted <u>Rear Admiral of the Red</u>
<u>Horatio Nelson created Duke of Bronte, social status indeed</u>

<u>Would our untouchable hero a touch of vanity this feed</u>
<u>Surely reeling with personal honour blotted copy book creed</u>
<u>He stole, against his adored fine character, another man's wife</u>
<u>'Twas Naples in Italy where began this twisted unwise strife</u>
<u>With Lady Emma Hamilton in 1799</u>
<u>Began his love affair disgraceful to entwine</u>
<u>This dishonour shocked England and his loving wife</u>
<u>His reputation would never recover for the rest of his remaining life</u>
<u>Behaviour so incompatible with the naval honours he'd aquired</u>
<u>For was he not the greatest man great England most admired</u>

Aboard HMS FOUDROYANT with cuckolded husband sad
Sir William and Lady Emma Hamilton and Nelson mad
Nelson hero valiant so smart with victory and sword
Unlukely smashed untied their marriage unity accord
As with Lady Hamilton danced with passion all the night
Her pained husband hopeless mourned his marriage flight
Our hero Horatio flawed, dalliance and dishonour rife
Severing ties with Frances to give her sadness and strife
His only child from out this union Horatia was born
But King and England did not approve
In England it caused a major storm
January 29th 1801
Their child was born
Her life begun
After her father this child was named
What greater honour
What greater shame
This child caused his first marriage to break
Poor Lady Nelson and England's adulation shake

But a naval hero further embue
As honoured Vice Admiral of Blue

Later back on consignment in 1801
On HMS ELEPHANT-with Captain Foley next battle begun
Independant in the Battle of Copenhagen victorious Nelson fly
Having disobeyed orders putting telescope to blind eye
Another honour amassed for England's naval hero's battle won
Viscount Nelson of Nile and Burnham Thorpe
In May 1801

But in January 1802
<u>Lady Nelson separated</u>
<u>Acknowledging her marriage with Nelson Through</u>

Even greater honours in May 1803
Made Commander-in-Chief of Mediterranean Fleet at sea
But tragedy would strike in 1805
When our greatest hero would not survive
Anticipating disaster his eyes could not his only infant leave
Fearing this sweet cherubic child an orphan soon bereave

Nelson his only child adore
Sweet Horatia was now just four
Daughter of the passionate Emma
Left his honour in some dilemma
Countless times he bade farewell
The infants cot he would not leave
He had to hug her again more times
As tears dropped down upon his sleeve

He had a premonition
This time 'twould be his last
He'd cast his eyes upon his child
Fearing death near battle's mast
Trafalgar would be his last sunrise
Upon his sleeping, sweet and only child
He must lasting feast his eyes.

October 21st 1805
Was the last sunrise he'd see alive
ADMIRAL NELSON with Captain Hardy on VICTORY HMS
Himself so bright so smart in Admiral's dress
Viewed the horizon at Cadiz in Spain
Weather, wind and sea surge scan
Every inch a practical sailor this genius man
Soon the silence gunshot broke
Every man to his station took
All keen to obey their hero, never forsook
His strong words their pride uplift
To have him in command their greatest gift
"England expects every man to do his duty"
This they'd do with honour impunity
There'd doubtless be injury, death and pain
Nelson repeat to his men so loyal again
Nelson in command the battle wildly rage
His brilliance on the wing, riven with sage
His inspiring words he alone did pen
Would be inspiration to his valiant men
" England Expects Every Man To Do His Duty"
Sudden see Villeneuve flag on Bacentaur beauty
Victory and Royal Sovereign approach the Spanish Franco fleet

In two straight lines to break the enemy line complete
Straight to the flagship Bacentaur Victory does attack
Seeing the flag of Villeneuve Nelson had the knack
500 muskets into the French flagship stern
Then double broadside that ship devastate in turn
The blood the smoke the wrecked riggings in action
Men shouting, guns blazing, sails flapping, devastation
Redoutable then Victory nearly seal its fate
Their decks were nearly touching in rage of battle take
But Temeraire appeared in nick of time
Crashed into Redoutable
And pushed her out of line
A shot was deftly fired from Frenchman
Up in the Missen high
Nelson's shoulder a perfect target through the smoke
From up towards the sky
In his uniform spectacular
A brilliant sight full
Ribbons and medals and hat elaborate to cull
His men well knew, below deck Nelson never flee
Always overseeing action in battle out at sea
He stood on deck his band of brothers urge
Lets pound them with another surge
Always leading from the front
This gallant brave now bore the brunt
Felled to the deck to great dismay
Just as the enemy routed away
This man who sword in hand
And warrior above all
Here on Victory stricken
Aware Almighty's call
Carried gently down below

Dr Beatty saw no surgical wonders do
Hardy his Captain kissed him on his cheek
As precious blood from the precious body leak
They never left him 'til the end
For everyman his every friend
Gradual gunfire now subside
As brave Horatio bare alive
But he knew the battle won
10 enemy ships were captured
The French and Spanish done
Never again to challenge British navy gun
But this brave brave Horatio won
But also sacrifice our noble admiral brave
That nothing in this world could he anyway save
Injured a blood vessel and his spine quite high
'Twix calm and agitation
It took three hours to die
"So kind so good so obliging a friend we never had"
Said his crew of their Admiral Nelson sad
" To dear Lady Hamilton be ye kind "
Then breath his body leave behind
At the Battle of Trafalgar

His body was preserved in a barrel of rum
Until it arrived back in England its end begun
Nelson honoured at Greenwich in devastated state
The nation mourn their brave brave hero Horatio's fate
State funeral   in London's Cathedral St Pauls
And burial in the crypt of fame, as the great befalls
Buried 1806 January 9
All England mourn this man so fine

But no invitation to either wife of hero great
Lady Nelson nor Lady Hamilton to mourn their dearest late
How come such a deficit could so devastating make
How could officials such a necessity forsake
That neither there to say goodbye
To the one they love, no one more cry
His sweet child weeps her father n'er see more
The toys he left she clutches close adore
Never was England's navy ever threatened again
By either vengeful country France or Spain.
England grieved their hero great and brave
They'd ne'er see like of Lord Nelson England save
No money gave this child to raise e'en tho' it was his blood
How could they scorn his only child when death had torn in flood
Those genes so precious grew with her
The hero's stamp they bore
The mother's love to nurture her
Would need financial core
No matter National Burial grand
If innocent child support not stand
So whilst England's brave had his duty done
England no duty gave to Nelson's little one
God Bless Nelson's Spirit brave
On Victory ship did England save
Sent French and Spanish ships to flee
1805 die a hero at sea
Courageous Nelson praise evermore
For this English hero we all adore

BMB-M 2005

ALLEGRO IN THE MAKING

The Classical Music Game

Two little girls set out to play the fiddle
Rebecca and Emma with fun hey diddle diddle
4 more little friends were duly found
And a Suzuki teacher to tune the sound
To teach these tinies with a mission
Amid clatter and toys and indecision
Their ages 3 to 7 range
Their mothers joined the lessons strange
And tried to avoid a gossip sneaky
Whilst glued intent on fiddlers squeaky
Well you'd truly be amazed
To learn that from this jangle crazed
Little squeakers good emerged
And critics opposed were quickly purged
All achieved mid laughter fun
Then music careers had just begun
Rebecca and Emma climbed grade by grade
As squeaks and errors began to fade
And within three years were on grade 5
Eager to pass with work did strive
A little practice every day
Big sisters also play
And all sang in Town Church choir
Divine sound soaring all admire
As the lovely bells familiar rang
The sweet voices of Christians sang

This did pave the young musicians way
As they practised their music every day
A family orchestra emerged with musical bond
The musical fun soared far beyond
Then came the crunch not fond
Not with fiddling bound pretend
But a fiddler must comprehend
Before the musicians head is crowned
Grade 5 theory rebellion found
Grade 5 theory unspeakably dull
From cadenzas and crochets this knowledge to cull
Rebecca took a stand at first sighting
'Twas not for her, flung books to flighting
No way would she acquire the urge
To take this boring learning purge
She'd flung it out at first cliff spot
My how it made her temper hot
When Emma felt this breezy draft
She also thought the book was daft
Joining hands with sister tough
Rebellion rife the boat did luff
Flung the boom in a mocking jibe
As mother's ego took a dive
To supersede impasse confused
Require much skill and tact she mused
"Would a game have more appeal?
She tentive put to sparky feel
" Rather!
Promise Mum we'll not give fuss"
We give that idea 90 plus
Playmates went gladly out to play
Amongst tall yellow buttercups and lengthening hay

To run in tall grasses swish their faces
As with labrador they play lets-beat-you races
To make daisy chains adorn each other
With sisters two there was no brother
Sarah and Charlotte bathed with each
As they frolic on Petit Bot beach
And laugh and shout when out of reach
Guernsey little Isle divine
On warm and sunny day sublime
Their sisters they did taunt
Too sloth for theory they did flaunt
You silly girls theory you must learn
There are notes you must discern
Sarah was a flautist fine
Charlotte's clarinet so divine
You can't stay at grade 5
If you wish your music thrive
Stretching for her pad to sketch
Mamma also paints did fetch
She'd have her art to twiddle
Or they'd rebel and stop the fiddle
Started toying with a game and bits
To remove the dull and bore for kids
Orchestras and instruments scatter
Amid composers heads that matter
And currency was music notes
And these on paper made to float
Ten works for composers 28
A brief life account of their life's fate
She sketched
At beach and boat and field
In the Forest Guernsey

This game to yield
And sailed to Islands Sark and Herm
Sketching with children
With Daddy at stern
Divine sparkling Island waters
Such fun in the sailing quarters
All great fun when Daddy had the time
To spare from eye Surgery
When in rest and best recline
Mamma too a doctor but needed holiday relief
To give time to their daughters four
Who they much encourage and adore
When Mamma had drawn up her plan
What activity in the house began
Drawing of composers and painting papers
Amid much laughter and teasing capers
Children's friends joined in the fun
Allegro's life had sure begun
Some with scissors some with glue
Activity engendered by the enthusiastic few
Even Daddy added currency paint
To distinguish crochets from quaver quaint
Six colours helped each from another
As six notes there are of value to cover
Green semibreves for 4 beats last
Whilst minims for only 2 beats cast
Crochets spread a single beat
As 'twere a second on clock to meet
A quaver is but crochet half
And passes twice as fast
Demi quavers half of that more
And demi semi quavers half that score

And race along so fast in speed
Only just possible your ear to feed
Now by lucky chance each of these notes
Fits the face of a dice
Six notes perfect
six perfect suffice
Currency to handle and a dice to throw
Now to make a game round it
For every child to know
Composers sat around the board 28 in all
To gain their ownership the players goal
One of each colour complete the set
And prize of winning there begett
The board scattered with knowledge to learn
By painless familiarity subliminal discern
The dice also for the musically able
Proceeds the player to a quiz book table
This book filled with serious music term and form
And guiding words for scales and such adorn

Playing the game

The mock up they'd all glued and painted
Now to play and become aquainted
So family six set down to play
And enjoy the simple game
Mid all the musical array
This fun and learning frame
By simple colour and number
To allow those of poor reading skills
To play with advanced and learned

In this game of gain and spills
Each player had a music instrument to move
around the board
And at double throw of dice
Given music money spend afford
Tchiakovsky Rachmaninof and Mozart
Beethoven and Brahms
Soon familiar with these complex names
Brought big sister laughs and qualms
The winner boomed the trumpets loud
The fun was there as colour crowd
It was a game
It really worked
Not just a Mamma's dream
To learning shirk
These children were now picking up
The stuff they had not wished to learn
Enveloping their eager minds
In fun no bore return
Quickly learn the values
By colour and number sought
And subliminal absorb the symbols
In playful method taught.
"It works!" she sudden shouted
Jubilant her spirits triumph
"This game is good, it really works
And knowledge easy come enough"
Play went on and none were bored
Some fortunes dipped and others soared
And those who'd not a semibreve thrown
Soon had the dice and better known
Orchestral discord amongst the ensemble

The flutes claimed Beethoven
And Elgars fortunes tumble
The drums thundered as their semibreves burst
To pay for Rimsky Korsakov
Flight of the Bumble Bee first
The woodwind clean idyllic sound
Pure lilting hit the height
As Verdi's Rigoletto
Purchased with delight
Mozarts Eine Kleine Nacht
Delighted the young fiddlers art
Handel's Water Music found
Indeed it came to drier ground
And Mendelsohn's gulls in Fingal's Cave
That Hebridean flight scene save
The Brandenburgs that beat from Bach
Would truly stir the soaring lark
Leningrad from Shostakovitch
Would boldly strike without a hitch
Mozart there to find repose
No greater favourite come n'er close
Sibelius Finlandia it was poetico
As the Fiddlers nobilmente and dolcissimo
The ringing of the Nibelung
Wagners grandeur forth was rung
And Purcell's St Cecilia's Ode
Was 16th century in its abode
Beethoven's Symphony 5 so grand
Excited maestoso this work in his hand
Player with Brahms accentuate
Hungarian Rhapsodies what finer fate
Vivaldi's 4 seasons brought sunshine and snow

Passionato and Tranquillo
Liszt's Liebestraume Poco or I lose
These quavers quiver me confuse
Weber's Invitation to the Dance
Doth players fortune much enhance
With Chopin's Fantasie Impromptu
Preludes and Nocturnes delight imbue
Pucini's Madame Butterfly
And La Boheme we know the best
Are the yearnings of the mass request
Elga's Enigma Variations
Stir the soul with good vibrations
Schubert's Unfinished and Trout quintet
Are joys we never will forget
Schumann's Piano Quintet in E Flat Major
May complete a set , I'll wager
Dvorak's New World inspires me with hope
To win this game , or I'll sulk in a mope
Tchiakovski's floating erudite
With Swan Lake ballet I take my flight
Hadyn's Emperor and Lark quartet
His genius my fortunes could now elect
Britain's Young People's Orchestra guide
Could bring many minims to my side
Eventually a winner of jubilance and zest
All stood up and cheered
She was the best!
It really was fun and worked they all agreed
And they learned masses of music without pain or heed
The music had sifted subliminally home
Without attention and none of the moan
Hurrah the idea had really hatched

And tuned to Mamma's thoughts
It really matched.

We then took it skiing to Andorra
With 7 aboard had laughter great
Keeping evenings after supper alive
With musical interest and fun and drive
But neither seen in pursuit of fun
Allegro's intent capturing the sun
People thought this game could go far
What a fun and learning star

One person wished this project invest
His kids loved it when he made the request
Quotes prepared for such a daunting plan
But so insistant was this man
The art work and 28 biographies fine
Took 2 years of hard work by Mamma and Flowline
These printers were both thorough and kind
So hundreds of visits she did'nt mind
Still more work for trade marks and patents
With Boult Wade and Tennant the elected agents
But the shallow investors after promises grand
Disappeared at first sneeze
leaving Mamma a desolate stand
The let down of the project caused distaste and alarm
They'd have to sell beloved
Bourg de Bas farm
The beautiful thatched house
Was quickly sold to others
Our misery at parting from house and Curly dear
From sweet Gracie our help soon came far too near

We kept some peach glass houses
And a cherished bit of land
To remind us of the happy times
When things got out of hand
With artwork and copyright
And patents vast expense
We'd have to leave our gentle home
To cover cost immense
Allegro was for family fun and learning justified
Especially for bright little Becca who reading had defied
Mamma had no illusions about a game for market made
Only Michael's insistence had we ever prepared this grade
Therefore to back out at the time the game was total ready
Was truly reprehensible and refused the ship to steady
We'd have to live in St Peter Port with eye practice close at hand
But we were used to country life and speading o'er the land
So profit from the house in hand and children off to England
We made Allegro work ourselves with zest and care command
Sarah at Southampton University, English and early music to master flair
Charlotte off to Sherborne School fortunately a great friend there
Both had been at Ladies College in Guernsey educationally sound
Rebecca loving Croft House School Dorset not so far away 'twas found
Emma starts her prep school, expensive cloaks flung on the floor
She soon met Lucy she'd met in Guernsey, a friend to share the dorm
So small house room adapted and looked very smart
Just to be happy is life's major art
Take disappointments and treasures
And with philosophy move
Never get stuck grovelling in a grove

Keep cheerful, not tearful if fortune's
Delivery at this moment seems not kind
Just remember family's health and
Welfare the only thing to bring to mind
And we'd had such happy times in
Precious Guernsey to be thankful
Extraordinary quality friends and
Lovely ophthalmic practice grateful
Now there was no going back
No wimping no defeat no back track
We simply pick up all the pieces
And behind strong shoulder bear
And forward march with song and fun
For what is there to fear
Although no real intention to feel the market place
By his savage break of solemn word
We'd step forward with full Grace

Production

Bradford Box Makers were alerted
To produce the finished games
Buying in the dice and boards
Moving pieces, plastic frames
3 months on 500 complete
Smooth wrapped and shiny neat

Sales

How to sell the ordered mass
No experience there alas
A mockup box sent to Mrs McGuiness
She ordered 3 dozen for
Hamleys when finished
Another 6 on sale or return
At Just Games
Hardly jubilance burn
Leaving 458 to sell
It seemed an enormous chiasm to fill
Publicity, publicity we needed much publicity

Publicity

In London a friend we shewed the game
Delighted, she up with an idea came
Suzy Menkes of the Express
Would love this game, it her impress
"Yes indeed" she quickly said
October 1980 printed and read
She'd wanted all our children and husband beside
To be pictured with the article to glide
But Becca and Mamma only to hand
Jenny Nesbit writing, did quite understand
After all who better
For Becca's dyslexia was the reason for the game
No better than a picture of the same
Suzy Menkes gave us a nearly half page
A great boost for the game she found
Educational and sage

Endless gratitude to her and Jenny
Without them the sales might not be any
Later the Sunday Telegraph a small paragraph of prize
And in December the Times a large picture raise
Amazement and rejoicing at each unexpected sight
Of newspaper write-ups
Helped Allegros better plight.

Collection of games
Mamma prepared the van for ship
But when she learned the price of trip
Honestly admitting it really was freight
She changed to roll-on roll-off car before too late
But driving to Bradford would be much less fraught
Realising the huge van was less practical than ought

A night with family in Stoneley in Surrey
Then off to Bradford to leave in a hurry
Up then to Connors factory yard
To leave pieces and composer cards
Then on to Bradford ahead at full speed
To collect the main boxes
Her spirits up-keyed
Exactly as tuned and planned
They were stacked high in the car
Strong hands well manned
Then when not a single inch to spare
But for the in to pack
Out came the manager
Sheets, looses rules for the box lid back
Sorry they'd not been printed on the lid
He profusely apologise

As an explanation she bid
And then a further shock
As she realised
They were the wrong lot
Poor man in a ruffle
Indeed an earlier printed version
To make redress need no coersion
Quick work table did arrange
To right these game rules all estrange
Another 2 hours of precious time
Was required to complete this line
Poor Mamma would have a problem she knows
To be at Connors by 5 p.m close
She hurtled down the M1 motorway
Nuneaton far too long to sight
She urged to car to faster
At muddles inefficient plight
Arriving there at half past five
Exhausted disconsolate and half alive
To find the main office locked
The men had left at five
Mercifully a director saw
Who sympathised her misery more
This joint it would not articulate
Allegro's fortunes amputate
The difficulties to sort
This awful blunder wrought
With the directors help, might reduce the thunder
He later came to minimise the blunder
He'd rounded up some men to work
They'd put this right and never shirk
Director went home to eat , so brief

But great was Mamma's state relief
At 8 o'clock this merry band
Of unskilled men to lend a hand
A tremendous atmosphere of work and fun
High spirits and jollity begun
One stirring glue these rules to fix
Another sorting money mix
Collating coloured counters
280 a box
Soon make like a cross eyed fox
Of different coloured must exact
They did with patience, hard work tact
Some did the box lid
Some plastic wrapping
In the great effort
To do the packing
At 11.30 p.m. car loaded burden finished
Gratitude enormous
Spirits undiminished
Cheerful waves from all those merry faces
Generosity and fun their dear hearts graces
Mamma will forget them never
These kindly folk their kind endeavor
She left a box for the Christmas raffle
"You've wonderfully rescued
From awful Kafuffle"
Again along the motorway with boxes packed so tight
She sudden another pannick
Empty tank no petrol sight
She took her off the motorway
To find a hamlet small
And parked by a police station

And explained to policeman tall
Hm! Hm! he said I think I see
How dangerous that packing be
I cannot see thou hast reflection
From your mirror rear deflection
"How do I find petrol here at night"
She asked so gentle so polite
"The AA man will 2 gallons supply"
I'll phone the request if you standby
But have you a nice cup of tea
Its late at night for a lady such as thee
Petrol placed and tea drunk
Another Christmas raffle prize
To these kindly hunks
At 2 a.m. off she rallied
Back on the M1 motorway
Speed, she could not dallie
Another few hours to Stoneleigh
How she wished her darling by her side
But the eyes of Guernsey must come first
So alone in danger glide
At dawn at Geoff and Maggies
She quietly slipped in
Care not to wake with loud disturbing din
At breakfast she related her disturbing trail
To the amazed family related her tale
The final product inspected
Shewed the rules to be far too faint elected
So rush to the printers
Who agreed the job to do
So dear Maggy and mamma
Stuck another lot with glue

A dash up to London later that day
To deliver a triumphant 3 dozen to Hamleys
Hip Hip Horray!
After 2 years absolutely complete
Smooth bright blue shining neat
A host of work and slavery bound
Allegro
actually completed sound
Back on the mail boat to Guersey's sunny isle
Exhausted triumphant with a happy smile
Flowline were to complete the rest
The car took only a hundred boxes to the crest
A few days later Suzy Menkes kind release
In the Daily Express gave the boost to unfreeze
Guernsey Press two hundred Allegro games bought
Quickly sales of 500 fare
Hard work to keep a few spare
Channel television an interview sought
So Emma and some friends to the camera were now brought
To play a game while chats
To tell the islands the music game facts
Children busy wrapping to send by mail
Set to music advertisement trail
The Toy fair was imminent in January due
Essential to plan a display booth new
A winning start for the Allegro game
Lets hope its future fared the same
Christmas in Guernsey with Aunty Margaret dear
An acquired sweet granny had their affections clear
St Peter Port Church Mass at Midnight packed tight
Our four beautiful daughters in this brilliant choir
Made the joyous sound take idyllic flight

Every seat filled, every pew
Those standing not a few

London Toy Fair

Then off to the London Toy Fair
With help from Guernsey Press
With long blue streamers
Banners for Allegro to impress
Big photos of the family line
Playing the game
Having a happy time
Video from Channel News, screen ready
People running the stall all day steady
Family friends were such a support
Patient in catch buyers thoughts
Not many orders the usual tale
Would we make a single sale
But Pebble Mill T.V. Fair review
Had picked out Allegro amongst games new
Giving it a boost most hard
Shewing dice and composer card
The press girl came rushing to the stall
To describe our success and tell us all
We whooped surprised amazed
And in our delight a little dazed
We loved the toy Fair bright and exciting
And wished all success the market biting

American Toy Fair

Flushed with enthusiasm and some success sealed

We decided to go to the New York Toy Fair
To try Allegro's fortune's further afield
There in the basement of the Sheraton Hotel
We displayed Allegro our doubts dispel
Next to our stall was a squirter of water
Who maintained high spirits in our quarter
We noticed a tiny person
Little more than a child
Kept coming to view Allegro
Asking for a sample filed
We said please be patient
When we leave we'll give you one
But we've only three to last
'Til we take the jet home fast
Three days 'til we have done
But she did most persistent come
And we let her have from three just one
She was filled with great relief
She Metropolitan Museum buyer in chief!
And this great place 1500 ordered now
We were staggered and wondered how
A chief buyer so young could look
That we nearly vanished from her order book
New York was amazing bright
Like a chandelier strung out at night
We raced like speedy tourists
To capture every sight
We saw multitude of flags
As United Nations building enter
Smart Maceys leave with smarter bags
The statue of Liberty
The Met Opera Pavarotti saw

Verdi's Masked Ball
Sensational! costumes music adore
Time Square all those N.Y. places
Busy rush and rushing faces
Plates piled high with far too much
High quality cuisine but rest can't touch
Upon Martha Tygel at Carl Fischer
Briefly then did call
Leaving an Allegro for appraisal one and all
Affectionate farewells to our stall neighbours
Who whooped it up with fun
And wished them well with their hilarious
Squirter Gun!
So fast vanished our whirlwind 5 days
Back to Guernsey routine
Somewhat in a daze
Back to work to tend the sick
As doctors we were bound
The eyes of all we did inspect
When trouble hit that ground
The Guernsey folk are gentle
The Guernsey folk are good
But oh to stretch its shores
Twenty times from where they flood
With twenty more great Guernseys
Would the world much better be
And twenty less some other isles
Less Godly by the sea
For Guernsey is a Christian Isle
That suffered from Hitler much
Now bustling, thriving banking driven
Tourism, flowers fruit and such

Most warmly were we all embraced
When from Australia we moved this place
A traditional haven of beauty and peace
Our nautical activity much increase
Its off shore Isles a place to go
Even France for the day
A breezy blow
Much hospitality, much social sport and like
Music thrive as people dive and frolic beach and bike

Sales from the Earls Court Toy Fair London

To fulfill the few hundred orders
From the toy fair's order book
We'd have to make some more
For the stores do empty look
The orders made a thousand
To each that made a part
So make the stocks more buoyant
Bestowing Allegro's heart
This second edition ordered were soon complete
Smart and shiny blue and neat
Mamma once more she took the van
Across the channel fetch the pieces
To articulate the span
Our dear old doggy Jason
A golden Labrador most kind
Would keep lonely Mamma company
So the journey she'd not much mind
In their van amongst the truckies
With curtains tightly drawn
And felt quite secure

'Til the following dawn morn
Again soared up the M1 motorway
To collect dice upon the route
And Bradford Box tried harder this time
And the rules were not forsook
The two set out to reach Southampton
With boxes packed in tight
Just room for Mamma and Jason
With both n'er out of sight
At last arrived and door bell rang
Out pounced Sarah's eager gang
Who were to fill the boxes at the Uni
Daddy and family to guide the way
On our Charlotte's birthday
Amid the frantic funny fray
In the basement at the Uni
Pop music loud at ear
An assembly line established
With high spirits and hands the gear
Immense efficiency to dazzle
Frantic fingers in the frazzle
As the dexterous spun to fill
Empty boxes through the mill
All to be securely bound
Through the plastic wrapper
From Guernsey Milk Board found
What fun what glee and even glad
When we'd finished the thousand
We were all rather sad
Tea and sticky licky buns
Mere token for all that they had done
These gallant kindly jolly kids

A croquet cup them more fun bids
Packed again in the van to high capacity
Cheery waves from their smiles of glee
We took the lot to Flowline
Who put the lot in store
What a happy relationship
With this firm a three year score
They said I was the most charming one
With whom they'd ever worked
Calm reigned throughout this time
Of intensive proofs that never shirked
Most helpful, patient wise at every step
Of this enormous project
To make Allegro's fortunes most adept
Now period of back to work
I looked upon the needy eyed
Mother wife and doctor
Mamma's every moment tried
Tried to stimulate some
Interest in the catalogue brigade
Succeeding with Tridias
Fine shop in Bath's Cavalcade
Met. museum in America
And Miles Kimball did assure
They both loved Allegro
And would add it to their score
So wait patiently awhile
And soon good fortune
Could stimulate your style
And there it came most unexpected
From Carl Fischer most delighted

A few days later
Met Museum order came accord
And Allegro seemed so buoyant
Under spirits high she soared
Dear Keith Ruddy of Lloyds
Said "yes, for funds to fill voids"
Funds to get 2000 made
For Met Museum Allegro saved
Mamma packed young Emma's clothes
For Youth orchestra tour
Stacked the deep freeze full of food for
Rob her husband she adore
And set off for New York alone
With art work, patents and moulds
To talk business with Carl Fischer
Famous music publishers we're told
Sheraton Hotel did book a room
Much did she pack against the door
She did dislike hotels
No husband or doggy to feel secure
A day to spare a boat she took
Round New York Island with sunshine afloat
Monday morning reached Martha expedient

Who organised meeting immediate
All solved as the phone she lift
Next mornings work Walter Connor cut adrift
The lawyers work he cancelled
The lawyers work he did demand
The three met at his command
To draft a contract their intent
To sign at noon their minds to bend

The lawyer Walter Connor and Martha
Sat down to drill a draft with no-moans-after
Indeed this contract duly signed
With exceptional speed
But Mamma
No lawyer she find
She had to trust the deal was right
And really no flaw immediate could she sight
And the artwork and numerous moulds
Collected by Martha from Sheraton Hotel
Straightway 5000 1/2 U.S. 1/2 U.K.
Were put to press
To be produced without delay
And speed Mamma to taxi smart
To speed to plane before it start
Back to Oxford for an academic day
At Ophthalmic Congress
Where our main interest lay
Then to Rebecca's Croft House School
Where in Mid Summer Night's Dream
She was a Snug most cool
Then hasty to the Guernsey boat
Which takes from Portsmouth
A full 6 hour float
Exhaustion hitting the jet lag jag
Was giving Mamma an extra sag
Collapse imminent misjudgement imminent
And teenage wrangles now
Home to cause dispair
And ruffle ridges which were not there
Back to Guernsey with clinics galore
Children four

And no peace store
For now we'd moved from out the farm
Closer living brought faster alarm
Sarah's uni friends arrived by the score
With little sensitivity had one U.K. core
And caused family ructions and sadness within
This normally closely knit kith and kin
So the settling process was delayed
At the start of the holidays cofusion made
All this brought the hasty contract in poor light
For the lawyer threw up hands
When he first caught sight
Adverse issue did he appraise
To disturb Mamma's calm from its diminished phase
Another lawyer from Ladas and Parry
Mr Baillie seemed much wisdom carry
Who also agreed a missing clause
That normally protects the inventor's cause
From cranks and phoneys who make false claims
Who cause a flurry until rejected in shame
Such responsibility is carried by the firm
Not the poor inventor a very tiny worm
So ruffled tranquility
Once more phone mobility
The following week a three way hooked
From New York, in the middle of a clinic
Mamma's attention booked
With patients sitting in a line outside
She tried to cage her words but the meaning abide
For the artwork and the moulds
An offer was defined

And accepted mentioning the problems underlined
Carl Fischer no problems could forsee
So offered no apology
The problem was left therefore to brew
Maybe of no importance
But time would tell anew
Carl Fischer had themselves truly protected
But unfairly had their inventors welfare neglected
But really it was obligatory
To have a word or two dissected
Or so the lawyers felt was just
But how could we pursue this must
Silly wrangles getting nowhere
Undermined that glorious rush
Unbalanced contract unequal protection
Took the bloom from Mamma's flush
However Allegro all this while
Was laughing exuberantly
Not the faintest fear of guile
Amazing how its fortunes flourished
Wonderful articles the press to flourish
October- Women's Realm children's Allegro competition
Then BBC on Radio 4 Robert Williams recognition
5 mins on P.M. programme Allegro describe
This all went out on the hour of five
Woman and Home and Country Life
Harpers, Set to Music and again in the Times
The game was praised amongst their lines
Dear Guernsey Press again so kind
And ever grateful bring to mind
Also the Channel T.V. cover
Made Mamma blush

She felt herself a most
Unbusiness like Mother
And then to cap it hail
Amazement !
Third best seller in the Daily Mail
Martha and Walter Connor
Were thrilled with delight
Vindicated on doubts of might
Another 10,000 was ordered utmost speed
Only 3 months after the first lead
But sadly they'd not listened when
Mamma spotted Allegros too few
The shelves had to be filled for this product new
Lack of stocks for Allegro of such acclaim
Could stunt its growth and make it lame
But no longer in Mamma's hands command
She indicated to New York in vain,
Demand greater than stock
Response slow, poor advance to lock
So stocks arrived far too late
For the Christmas rush
Thereby stalemate fate
But nevertheles if handled right
It would stay at the top
In the marketing fight
More disruption from Boosey and Hawke
Who disliked big brother indicating
Where to use their fork
Disliked being told
To sell Allegro with firmer hold
So transalantic big brother began affect adverse
The gleaming product from anaemia could thirst

The heart beat first so strong
But slow response to stocks
Would trim this star before long

The lawyer prompted to take action
If contract not changed to satisfaction
If indeed Carl Fischer were ever late
Paying a dollar- per- box royalties
Eclipse could be their fate
Mamma was'nt sure what to do
Real sound advice came from remarkably few
Fearful of upsetting this shining star
But I had this opportunity
To stop this contract from afar
With no protection from cranks, safe
Eventually asked lawyer to stop this contract waif
So only nine months on
Mamma cancelled and it was gone
Carl Fischer was upset, 15000 had sold
As a classic for adults by the pool
Stop were told
Had 25,000 in the pipeline
In Spanish translation done
Now it was cancelled
Mamma's interest was not won
She would not budge from contract poor
She made this game for family fun
Anxiety would shade her sun
A million would not make her glad
If cranky people could sever sad
Better peace of mind and poor
Than all the riches feeling sore

Lawyers were most folks bete noire
Hardly music of Allegros choir
Therefore better finished and done
Than anxiety which gives no fun

BMB-M 1982

The game hopefully inspired all yoiung musicians and our 4 lovely daughters.
Perhaps they ealize that even Mothers can achieve something other than the
most important thing in their lives which
is devoting themselves to family happiness and emotional security of her
husband and children to produce strong resilient adults
All four passed grade 5 theory of music
Emma is a singer songwriter www.emmab-m.com
Mamma still owns the copyright of Allegro
Somebody found Allegro on sale in the Metropolitan Opera House New York
3 Oxford undergraduates sharing a house in Oxford University had Allegro
amongst their family games

DEBORAH BARTRAM

Child of genius

*A brilliantly funny script writer
who sadly died at 26 years old April 2003
from Anorexia Nervosa*

*Sweet child of destiny
Know you not your worth
For every writing is a brand new birth
Dwell not upon weak philandering father
Or bullying at school
For most are cowards
And some are merely fools
Think of the joy when you were born
Your parents ecstasy at this tiny form
Then to watch you grow in size and intellect
Such was your developed genius
You were never a child of love neglect
A special child
A bloom of spring
Funny words to make folk laugh and sing
But food doth feed to keep the hand alive
And worldly words upon the well fed body thrive
But now the petals shed your human breath
No more that hand o'er paper glides
But ideas and vision in your spirit still resides
Ideas that set the angels chuckling in their mirth
As gently bears this genius from confused and troubled earth*

The spirit lifts from frail frail petal shell
As angels bear to Heaven
Rescued from your starving hell
Sweet child of destiny
Now you know your worth
As your God welcomes you from confused and troubled earth

BMB-M

JOHN PEEL (RAVENSCROFT)
November 2004

A man born to cotton riches
Preferred less lofty to relate
The fine old man of spinning discs
Pop music his main fate

But he never never played my music
From emmab-m.com's hand
As he said he surely would
Maybe I was'nt a boy band
Or ever Irish origin could
He never did my sweet songs play
I always thought "another day"
But now he's gone from radio one
I guess it'll never be
Maybe because a distant cousin
I almost was you see
Family were less appreciative
Of his tangled American History
We'll never hear his droll wit more
Or his tousled look to see

He DJ'd in California
As Liverpool accent found
At the time of Beatlemania
His fledgling career gained further ground

But he never etc

He was a goodly family man
Sheila and 4 children he adore
In Suffolk mud he walked the dogs
"Home truths" on Radio 4

But he never etc

He championed the underdog
On radio one at night
He gave some scruffy lads some air
And set their star in flight

But he never never etc

In far Peru his heart did fail
Quite sudden when in full regail
And millions mourn this man quite rare
To spin the pop/rock his great flare
But he never never

This iconic music man
Will now be greatly missed
He'll spin his pop/rock discs in Heavan
As angels lyres assist

BMB-M

Just William
It's fun to be a child of five

Its fun to be a boy of five
To run and jump and feel alive
And swim in pool
And go to school
For numbers and reading
To play with friends
Wresting and Kicking
(balls of course)
I can climb
And carry without spilling
And eat without a mess
Well not too much
It was tipping
I can dress and undress
Even tho' I often miss a trick
And lose a sock or two
But it usually turns up
So daft
Two in the other shoe
Silly me!
And as for those shoes
They always make me late
They're always on the wrong foot
However hard I concentrate

I swing upside down

Like big boys do
Then fall on my head
And cry instead!
I draw a lovely picture
With flowers and kisses
And numbers and letters
And words with near misses
Then spill my milk
With my silly sleeve
Then spoil the picture
And cry with peeve
I think I can do everything
Then find I cannot do
But don't give up, says Ganny
Keep plugging on
You'll see it through
And what is time
And how is it lost
It really is a worry
Clocks and watches a mystery
And everyone in a hurry
Where is yesterday
And how long 'til tomorrow
Yesterday, tomorrow
And names of months are hard
I simply can't remember them
Even after seeing words upon a card
And why does food get everywhere
And not stay in its place
I feel I'm sticky with splodges
From my shirt to over my face
On really bad days!

I cuddle a toad and give Ganny a fright
Why wont she hold him
It can't be right
Neither does she like my wriggly worms
I collect when Ganpa digs the land
She pulls a face
No thankyou dear
I'll never understand
In Marti's horse muck
I slodge and slide
Why is Ganny so fussy
About smelly boots inside!
Marti is my great big friend
Around the trees I race
For windfalls on the ground
And feed her huge and greedy face
She tries to gobble my hands
And that would be a disgrace
Whilst eating those I've found

Ganny seems not much to like
My manners at the table
But I can assure you now
It's the best of which I'm able
But I do get my tools in a twist
Who ever thought of knives and forks
To tangle tiny fingers and fists
But Chinese bits of litlle stick
Are even worse they say
So knives and forks
Will most probably have to stay
I know that praying to Jesus

Will help to make me good
But couldn't He try a little harder
To make my mischief understood

My words and numbers
Are coming on a treat
Wish I was'nt such a fidget
And could sit still upon my seat
But teacher does'nt mind
As long as we are quiet
And don't race round like maniacs
Creating a wild school riot

And I wish I were'nt a Jack-in-the-box
And keep coming down from bed
Somehow my naughty feet keep taking me down
And I cant train my silly head

After bath and bed and story
To Jesus I fervent pray
Ask Him to make me better
And my friends with whom I play
Especially Joshe who's nasty
And kicks when no one's there
He's going through patch that's bad
But bruises hurt and make us sad
Please Jesus look the other way
When I kick him back
Cos that's what my sense does say
I pray for all my family
And my Mum whom I adore
Who gives me love that boundless
Lots of pressies and much more

I pray for horse and pussycats
My soft and purry friends
We always love each other
And will 'til this big world ends
I pray for Jabez and wish he were my brother
For if he were I 'd never play with any other
And please bring him to live a bit closer
So we can play most every day
For there's never any friend with whom I'd rather play

I love my grandpa in the garden
We dig, weed, cut and clear
So nice flowers and cabbages
Grow in the ground next year
And whilst you read my few words here
You should in mind bear
He'd never manage this garden
If I were'nt working here

Ganpa plays and kicks a ball to me
And we pick some flowers for Ganny
And fill Martis bag with hay
She watches us so canny
Another thing I love to do
I stir the painting colours round
Until me thinks a gold brown found
Then I know
God stirred the rainbow
Whilst near the bright warm sun
Until he painted me golden brown
When my skin had first begun

BMB-M

ELIZABETH-SARAH

Elizabeth was a sweet pretty kid
On parenthood she lifted lid
For indeed she was the first
Until 3 more upon them burst
Black curls round cherub face unfold
Then these turned quite cornfield gold
Her gentle nature and her grace
Always sweetest smiling face
Eldest of much adored four
Infinite indulgence upon them pour
From the start bright thrived at school
Preferring words to numbers cool
Born in London, Barts no less
With Grandparents from 4 months
They loved and caress
As parents did in hospital slave
As housemen medical training made
She was but six when to Australia flew
A rich bush life in country new
She rode her pony with fun much
The pickle Pinnochio who knew her touch
Schools loyal salute the jack
Rough immigrants from U.K. back
Pony, piano, flute excel & sisters three
Life amazing life a spree
Simple, sweet, happy country wild
Family close no frills undefiled
After seven years once more to move

For the 6 to Guernsey clove
Learning the joys of the sea close by
Golden beaches hearby lie
Ladies college rigid and prim
But to Southampton Uni at 18 begin
Then to Australia and New Zealand
She and Spanner work
From job to job, never to shirk
Wedded bliss to him forsake
These vital steps she could not take
With Kings Consort and Robert King
And Academy Ancient for 15 years ring
But then diverge to pastures new
Alexander technique to treat the few
Training done to Edinburgh went
Where several years she spent
Her fun approach much following find
As folk learn her healing hands so kind
Brought plenty pupils with aplomb
University posts she gradual build
And part-time in beloved Guernsey filled
Altho' many a suitor had wished
To step into marriage- she never dished
She says she's happy and merry seem
But hardly the life her parents dream
But hark a wind change we now see
Ian is acceptable and maybe husband to be
If so with roses garland love
With copious Blessings from above

BMB-M

MARY-JULIA-CHARLOTTE

Uncomplicated brisk and focused yet
Of tender heart we did beget
Practical hardworking
And of science slant
Nothings impossible, never say cant
Her husband James an instant knew
This man for me and music the cue
'Twas first week at Oxford and her dice was cast
Her beauty bewitching to win him so fast
He the conductor
She in the choir
With cupid's magic ignite the fire
Scholarship Queens Guide Oxford to go
From Guernsey Agri Forestry to bestow
At 21 married to soulmate James
At New College Oxford of musical fame
Then she to McDougal
They lived in Windsor flat-times were frugal
First selecting from British graduates
Her peers of distinction much to fluctuate
Tiring of stop-go too much then too little
Finally to market sales and quibble
Choc. cakes yeast and flour selfraising
She decided money was not for her grazing
Medical drew her, her parents to follow
No earnings would leave both pockets hollow
But medicine she must with her fantastic man
Frankie teaching and baby Alex came

So medical student wife and mother be
As 5 years of study quickly flee
Meanwhile another Fowler child
Baby Luke more nappies piled
Frankie father teacher husband kind
Working for exams whilst food and children mind
Julia eventual doctor became
First general practice for this dame
But stresses with family incompatible
And sorting criminal element alone at night
Surely did realize impossible plight
Set forth on pathway difficult radiological
More physics and study
Whilst Frankie rose educational
Head of sixth at Brentwood School
Alex and Luke St Pauls Cathedral sing
Where 100 years before Shaw voices there ring
Alex Carribean a challenge ocean sailing bring
MOD scholarship & medicine at Barts
Whilst Luke rowing team & architecture heart
These musical children intelligent emerge
From their parents dedication and disciplined surge
Julia worked awhile at beloved Barts
Which her parents sought to save over decade past
Great Ormond Street St Thomas' and Cambridge all attended
Whilst her fellowship obtained mid exams extended
At last consultant grade
Exams at last to the past now fade
Frankie now to Highgate deputy rise
Soon to a headship no surprise
This wonder man had much sacrifice
Cook brilliant husband father much suffice

But now his special qualities show
As great responsibility he easy tow

Highergate School musicians great to seed
Tavener and Rutter great to heed
Then to Bedifordia as Hatfield Heath sold
To accommodate day boys in family fold
Voices both broke within a year
Fantastic years at St Pauls ended clear
Now to rowing rugby and cricket
Renovations and consultant job a new wicket
Then to a major headship for her man
Thought dedication and astonishing ability
Brings her another doctorate from cerebral agility
Godbless this family four and wishes grant
Rose petals kind their lives to plant
Imagine that little one first on the scene
40 years back came so easy and clean
Effortless sweet content and exquisite
A second little miracle her family to visit
An easy childhood bonny and biddable
3 sisters to have fun with energy amicable
Dark titian and beauty be
Charming, hardworking, wife, Dr, mother all three.

BMB-M

SUSAN-REBECCA

An exquisite baby
With a dusting of golden hair
Upon her tiny head round
Grew to be a right little madam
Stamping tiny feet upon the ground
She suffered dyslexia
Whilst of fine intellect mind
Could reduce a class to chaos
If boring teaching she find
Fine violinist and contralto voice
But reading left her with no choice
Fun and observant with multitude of friends
Great at sport and acting all which made amends
For the beastly reading
For which her mother made a game
Allegro for this and younger child alone
To learn the theory of music
Reached acceptance, nearly fame
At 13 the dyslexia vanished and her confidence
Soared to sky
At last she saw those words, quite still
And then she felt that she could fly
She loved her time in Wales
And from boarding to comprehensive school
Loved her pals from the mountains
As her eyes had lost their scales
Secretarial at Oxford
With a year in USA

Met Simon her Oxford cricketing teacher husband
To protect her from the fray
BBC foreign programme
Then Capitol Radio
Then television production
With two kiddies on the go
Gregariously collecting
A multitude of friends
Busy busy work and social fun
A balance hard P.R. work lends
Fantastic friend, mum, wife
This busy bee you'll find
Now getting into films
Of main promotional kind
Watch this spot with husband Si
These two together
They will climb high
With their darling lively Saskia and Jabez two
Bringing them headaches and magic
Each and every year through.
May God's Blessings guide their destiny sweet
And all their hopes and wishes meet

BMB-M

MARGARET-OLIVIA-EMMA

She was an Aussie born this child
When Royal Shakespeare were in Oz
Twelfth Night and Winters Tale
Superb of minimal props because
On tour in far Japan and more
A delighted audience always score
As temperatures swelter Melbourne Streets
In February folk pale as heat soar
This child emerge so sweetly fresh
Dark hair, and cheeks aflame
Sweet sisters wanted her to name
In Ozzy bush wild she was raised
Then Isle of Guernsey family to graze
They went there when this child was three
To play the waves and splash the sea
To sail the boats and warmth to greet
Hospitality unsurpassed this pretty seat
In music she thrived like her sisters three
Violin, piano, voice and in Church choir on her knee
Then board on the mainland in Dorset mild
Then Oxford to study Mandarin filed
The music took a different turn
As composition she yearned
But health became difficult as allergy cloyed
And diet control favourite foods avoid
Later to Taiwan to poetry pursuit
But unhealthy industrial air attack acute
And back to England music pursue

A most important pop-song for Barts Hospital write
Which helped reverse Barts near destruction plight
Conspiracy against Barts the title propagate
Barts was saved in 1998
Until car accident health knocked anew
Pop singer songwriter her goal now
Including the classical injections vow
CD albums with videos aplomb
Website www.emmab-m.com
Then motherhood her focus change
Not together with the father arrange
To the states together to raise
But so brave in England, lone parental maze
Sweetest child made scene less hard
Love and belief renders kinder cast of card
This bundle of amazing love
A joy to all
Music grows and expands in length
Stll in pop idiom and operatic strength
Inspiration as a teacher noted
To this art she is devoted
As speed her fingers over Prokofiev keys
Her teacher wonders why not concert lease
It will come together as He plans
She is certain preach through music pop
And classic combined to cream the top
And belief in God is strong devout
Of this she bears not shred of doubt
This child has the Shaw talent
As he a chorister and violinist amazing
And a speedy tennis and tabletennis blazing
A friendly warm heart as friendship kindles easy

Fun eminating as he plays free and breezy
But they need a dear man to protect them now
Every child a father, every woman a man to vow
May God's Blessings guide these two
And kindly bestow their wishes as life pursue.

BMB-M

CHANNEL ISLAND SIEGE

There was a spot in the Channel Isles
"A jewel" in the sea towards France
In the last three years there've been dramas
Two aggrieved pros leading a dance
An Indian doctor and an aggravated vet
Inextricably caught in the Island's bureaucratic net
The former crossed swords and unwisely wrangle
With a tough hospital secretary with whom better not to tangle
Hithertoo this breed would know their place
And know doctors as their betters and not step out and face
But as social worker she had been trained to overpower
Those older and wiser
Any problems just pull down the visor
Another two decades would pass before safely handle
Their new found groundless power without scandal
But she effectively whipped the scalpel from this surgeons hand
Although he'd received an reference fine
With reliability underline
From Dr Riche of most respected Ophthalmic band
Devastating for the locum the Indian doctor now lamed
Worst of all cut by a woman
Who were to him inferior framed
But the Board of Health the woman backed
Who had this doctor virtually sacked.
His employers were at first supportive
Thinking unfair judgement could be rife
But when a fight in the operating theatre
He serious threat, incensed by this strife,

If anyone his surgery stop
He'd seriously would attack with mop
"No one can stop me" he shouted and stormed
They realized the situation had him derranged
And the owners withdrew their support, and now estranged
The law and the Board of Health duly informed
He must be on his way home his journey arranged
But this he vehemently would not do

One month later he refused to leave
His lent premises he barricaded with heave
Upon sound advice with a bobby to arrest
He was evicted lawfully as an obnoxious guest
But before this scandal
A vet incensed with a similar demean
Similarly stormed the Island
And used the Island's scheme
Of a "Clameur de Haro" upon the knees
To halt any grief which did displease
He knelt here
He knelt there
And sometimes in the air
Suspended from a crane
By the harbour
But suspended all in vain
He subpoenaed here
Subpoenaed there
Conducted own council
With neither success or flair
He chased poor magistrates
Their wigs all askew
Disturbing their dignity they always knew

Eventually safely behind bars he sullied
The Island would be no further bullied
No he could not on this Island
Set up as a vet
Restrictions were essential
To ensure balance met
Only those selected by the powers that be
Could practice as doctors or vets you see
But the upset Doctor decided to sue
But over the time limit and could not go
But the owners said yes we want the truth told
Let him take it to court
The truth must out
As well it ought
But the Island was afraid of another vet stand
And it was decided justice must be overruled
Incase the doc got out of hand
And went nutty like the vet
This situation could not let
So when the case came into court
The owners valued evidence was not sought
Their advocate's voice was under malfunction
Feebly allowed the rejected doctor get his satisfaction
So never was it brought to court
The reason the owner had him sacked
Was because what the Indian Doctor had intended
He just never could have defended
Fighting off all opposition
Porters and all
In the operating theatre
If they tried to stop his surgery all
Madness in the theatre was strictly out of bounds

No matter how the ego hurt
A patients interest must be found
But the Island saw a trouble maker
And thought the two to whom it had been good
Would surely surely have understood
And in the Island's interest
They must be quiet sacrificial lambs
As a thankyou for the happy years
On this dear happy Island and its sands
Their friend a fine eye surgeon
Had given a good report
For this Indian eye doctor for whom
Rejection now was sought
It was more a case of ego

Had his fortune now   deflated
He assumed it was his colour
That they had unfairly hated
Nothing farther from the truth
Amongst these kindly Island folk.

BMB-M

Gillian and Virginia
English Ladies
Suffolk's Genteel, devoted, loving sisters

Virginia and Gillian
So different in every respect
Had a deep affection which sweet families expect
It equalled that of marriage and of child
Caring and gentle, warm and mild
These beautiful talented daughters
The apples of their parents eyes
Virginia adoring her infant sister
From her very first tiny cries
Born of delighted parents,
An eminently talented furniture designer
Artist pargentist and architect
And most kindly hospitable mother
Elegantly tabled food delicious delect
Virgina wisp-like lovely dancer of ballet
Gillian exquisite up the piano keys sally
Virginia to Rada acting to find
Alexander Korda film spy in mind
In Return of the Scarlet Pimpernell
Intrigue and excitement story to tell
Operas, teaching drama and dance
Painting, embroidery lives to enhance
Artistry, intelligence and sweetness exude
Both enchanting their parents guests
With charming entertainment interlude
These talents raised funds for Spitfire drive

In 1940s war to keep England alive
In Haughley village hall a concert fine
These ladies helping fight Hitler malign
Ballet acting and piano keys play
To delighted audience eager Spitfire to pay
They knitted and parceled to troops in the War
Trying to save England which they all adore
No suitors ever measured parent's expectations
This gentility unsurpassed by marriage election
Always by their parent's side
Happily the decades forward glide
Until through melt of time and space
Their parents timespan end did face
Grieving their parents demise
These loving sisters drew ever closer
As dried each other's eyes
Many decades more in the same house, same land
As devout Christians lending a hand
Elegantly entertaining as befits English lady election
Superb cooks everything silver, fine china perfection
Both rode confidently to Suffolk hounds
Hedges and ditches knew no bounds
Gillian Vice president of Suffolk Agricultural Show
Encyclopaedic memory
Of all in Wetherden you'd ever wish to know
In cassock and surplice in Wetherden Church
Singing and reading no greater pleasure search
Virginia's dramatizing the Bible clear
Brought sudden life to the words writ here
Appreciating Suffolk seasons of primrose and corn
As the first Spring light and the wheatears form
Such kindness to each other and all they met
This placid life rarely grief fret

Transcended sweet mother child and brother
Every necessity smoothly cover
But age creeps fast
This could not last
After 70 years of Wetherden life
These two sweet ladies met medical strife
Virginia cruel Alcheimers disease decay
She sadly no more know which day
Many falls she then withstood
Sometimes found wandering on the road
And Gillian many infections fight
Met by modern medicine's might
In time required a carer's care
And crises well met if Mary there
Thelma, David and other village friends flocked caring
Did all they could to ease the problems bearing
Virginia was 90 when battle was lost
Gillian close by she loved the most
Dear Bubby had gone
But her spirit hovered near
She'd again care for her sister
Their affection so dear
Their close love would never die
Their loving parents too
Would be nearby
Bless this sweet love of this family strong
More of it would strengthen
This sad world we belong
May angels bear Virginia's sweet soul
To God's loving arms there
And Godbless and comfort sweet Gillian here

B.M.B-M 12.7.2008

Drusilla McLeod 1932-2007
The Intended Lady Of Dunvegan Castle

Skye
Drusilla beloved daughter of famed Shakespearean actor
And film star of 40 films in the 1920s
The great Sebastian Shaw now weeps
At Dunvegan Castle in the Isle of Skye
The Island weeps with John, Chieftan-intended
Dame Flora's kindly comfort arm extended
Distraught mother Drusilla weeps
Condolences receives
Her twins still-born
All were forlorn
These heirs Macleod
Never to breath and live
Their sweet mother
Never her sweet love to give
The shock it made this mother ill
And abound more illness still
Multiple miscarriages
Where shines the sun
As heir must come
A tragic loss and worse to come
To tragic cloud the marriage sun
John needs to train to sing
Both to Geneva bells do ring
But Cushings disease established cruel
On sweet Drusilla a veto fuel

Her doctors said to Geneva she must not
Balancing delicate hormones priority slot
Sadly to her dear love she sadly bade him go
She would follow when her health restore
Grieving his departure and her sweet babes
A newfound low her spirits enslave
She wept as she traced with her finger
Where the twin's name might be
At the end of the list of Chieftains
Of the Macleod family tree
She wept as she swept her fingers
O'er the Fairy flag case
Which ensured victory
When Macleods a battle face
She wept as she trod the round-garden dell
Through trim box edged paths
Tears on rose petals fell
She wept by the waters of Dunvegan Loch
As they gently lapped in sympathy her tears to mop
Found shivering weeping by the great trees, so cold
When the gong rang for dinner
In the castle so old
And now separated from her darling love
When she needed him close to care for his dove
And wished she'd not said
"Yes, you must go my dearest darling and learn to sing
With notes sublime to make my ears ring
With joyous sound our love to fare
And bring forth babes to make an heir"
And now he was so far away
His loving arm not there this day

Indeed not there where he should be
But already another did he see
Made quick more heirs to make
His sweetest love for sex forsake
And false husband dance the May
The dance of infidelity dishonour and dismay
When Skye heard a boy was born
To this false Macleod of honour shorn
Disapproval swept the Isle
And Dame Flora did not smile
When Drusilla heard the news
Astonished did first believe refuse
The love divine
He with whom her heart entwine
She must let go
But this her heart could never do
Wed for ten years she tender and true
No further marriage would she pursue
Yet he for ever more to wed
Another and yet another yet
Certainly by these his heirs ensure
But for restlessness he found no cure
The true jewel he'd traded for an heir
He'd attained that and one or two spare
But true peace of mind eluded with waste
For truth with honour requires good taste
Drusilla brought much joy to every life she touch
With warmth and kindness
Of which her nature much.
She never married more
But had friends by many score
In last year her sweetest friend
Welsh sheep dog Sophie, her heart to bend

In a crisis this dog adoring saved her life
Licking her face to allay the strife
In the very flat John and she first owned
Amongst their first shared treasures in London town

50 years on they both with cancer took
And within weeks they each their breath forsook
Her funeral was but a day before
His memorial was but a day more
They were united at death's door.
He'd waited for her and did tender implore
Forgiveness for his "heir search' harshness
T'ward she he adore
She understood his impossible situation
Which led to degradation
Changed from Wooldridge Gordon to Macleod in name
Gave obligation to produce an heir of name the same
For John Macleod of Macleod Chieftain proclaim
If no heir to follow he'd receive the blame.

Now cleansed
Now that his accursed body was thankful left behind
He'd be hers for ever their gentle hearts entwine
Her loving soul so readily forgive
They would forever
In sweet spiritual embrace now live

When the soft white whispy cloud is seen passing over Skye
Wafting gently towards Dunvegan Castle, sun high up in sky
They are watching gently, guarding folks on Skye
As hand in hand these sweet tragic lovers pass them by.

B.M.B-M 23.8.07

Alex the Brave
(Organ scholar with Cystic Fibrosis at Eton College)

Notes radiating from heart, head and hands
As rays from the sun on quiet sea and gold sands
From this genius held together with glue of powerful will
Quelling life's vicious medical storms to harmless still
Talent extraordinary on the keys
Organ Scholar and choral ease
Captured notice at Eton fine
At 13 he was scholar first in line
Intelligence, musicality, enthusiasm supreme
Burst sparkling upon the Eton scene
But
At birth he takes a savage blow
Cruel cystic fibrosis constrict breath flow
Infections, breathless coughing bouts
Plagues this child his years throughout
Living upon the cliff edge of life
With matchless will to fight the strife
Never a grain of self-pity found
Maturely tackling, doctors confound
Courage immense mid splutter and wheeze
Ever smiling courteous breeze
Pulmonary function to a third restricted
Breathing capacity severely afflicted
Fun and fast in all endeavour
No excuses, no lessons sever

Spirit magnificent
Courage immense
Sprints athletic o'er the keys
Seek excellence intense
As approaching Bach's Magnificat
To conduct the Eton Choir sound
Near fatal infection struck another blow
As in intensive care himself he found
Doctors fought keep life above the line
Gradual the pale wan face colour redefine
Once more bouncy wreathed in smiles
Soon his tennis planet
Was bouncing up the miles
He discharged immediate as upright stand
This steel of inner strength waved his hand
To hospital staff who'd pulled him through once more

Off to Eton School rehearsals explore
Scooting merrily down its corridors length
The more he moved
The greater his strength
The musicians assembled with Alex to sing
Ever their admiration bring
Waving his baton, coaxing groups with his arm
The orchestra and choir
Create music with calm
The sound rise in magnificence
Bach himself would sure approve
This frail stick of determination
Sweet harmony to sooth
Between intravenous antibiotics
To many surgical ports

Tablets galore and special foods
This willow give support
The wilting stem given fibre
By this tower of inner strength
He waves in trumpets, cellos
And strings of lesser length
The voices rise and fall
Notation by Bach fixed
The fervour in the boys
By admiration transfixed
This frail sick brilliant boy
So young yet strong of heart
Conducted Bach so well
Their attention focused every part
Alex has his tennis ball
Sphere of constant inspiration
Effortlessly bouncing energetic agitation
Being bowled for summer's cricket
When clouds mass overhead
From hand-to-hand constant ossilation
Suggesting hope and sun instead
His tiny furry planet
Reflects his spirit
Of great depth and power within
Perpetual motion never ending Grace and hope
His immense perpetual spin
This giant spirit commanding
So frail a frame
Conducts Bach for the actual day
With great gusto
To beat setbacks again
A performance brilliant

To tear stained applause
Their hearts wrenched
Cystic —Fibrosis- fight-back the cause
Show me not the rubbish
The media portray
For Alex is the true HERO
We'd crown upon this day

B.M.B-M 26.1.08

Judi Dench (Williams)

Amazing actress Judi
Brother Jeffery inspired
Teeming with talent
These two abide
Australia 1970 we first viewed this acting feast
Royal Shakespeare company
Touring Japan and Far East
Twelf Night and Winters Tale
On Melbourne stage
Their greatness hail
Few props, stark and bare
Yet we immediate
Recognised greatness here
At this moment Michael Williams
Arrived to take her hand
Off to Ayres Rock to propose
Where the great red rock stand
The love of her life
Another actor fine
Australia romantically their lives entwine
To a marriage happy strong they bind
Continuing then the Aussie tour
Australia astonished at such fine view
Indeed all must follow this acting new
Follow each and every act
Great variety and quantity
The titles stack
Never a scandal

Always Dench humour to the fore
Great memory of lines
Directors respect to greatly score
The older she gets, the greater the age
The more they want her on film and stage
And if only he'd not hidden in Stratford for family
That amazing brother Jeffery would be equal fame
But a devoted family man cares not for equal name
But maybe you'll still strike lucky
His wondrous booming great voice to hear
If in his old age you are lucky to be near
His poetry and Shakespeare balanced fine
Exquisite diction for every line
Emma B-M's Operatic glory the team complete
Here you'll savour incomparable Dench replete
Another seat of talent emerge
As Judi's child Finty her acting surge
So more treats in store from this famous family yet
As the brilliant Denches approach their warm sunset

12.2.08 BMB-M

Joan Mary Eileen Ingpen
1916-2007

A humble start as shipping clerk with quill
Talent on Royal Academy piano fulfill
ENSA then Sir George Solti on her new agency book
Borrowed 100 pounds the cost she withstood
Astonishing memory, hard working, precise
Encyclopaedic each aspect of new opera singers concise
When there was sickness and new gap emerge
Flew such as Pavarroti from far, to world stage to burst
Joan Sutherland, Kiri te Kanawa and many more
This magnetic woman casting agent
Matching new ready talent to score
Covent Garden then Paris Opera and later to the Met.
Climbed as an icon the highest opera set
Over world opera stages she held great respect and command
Introducing ready "locum stars" when sickness demand
2 broken marriages and finally actor Sebastian Shaw
For forty years the man she could finally bond and adore
Spreading her genius to adorn stages afar
At 91 departed undoubtedly, herself, a star.

B.M.B-M 23.1.08

Rev. Canon Ronald and Myrtle Hares (1908-2007)

Was there ever more Saintly than Myrtle and Ron
Missionaries in India 1920s where first they were gone
Dedicated to their Lord and nursing care of the poor
Inspiration to all with service their work's core
Great preach from pulpit when to Beccles returned
Then to Guernsey no better folk could have yearned
Finally to Hasketon in Suffolk to preach
That village now holds remains as to Heaven they reach
For now Myrtle has joined him her long wait is gone
Their great love together has now joined the throng
Their kindnesses legendary their faith shone bright
Here is the true couple of Christ's warmth and light

B.M.B-M

A carol

The nativity scene lit by candles
Angels and a star
Mary Joseph and the Babe on hay
Shepherds, Kings have come so far
Cattle warm and gazing
Found in simple stable shed
Aglow with sweetest joy
A manger for his bed
His eyes wide bright with wonder
To see this earthly scene
People kindly welcoming
No simpler birthplace been
Mary sighs relief that
Her babe so safe arrive
Attentive to his every need
Ensure sweet infant thrive
Gently wraps and cuddles
This small treasure, God's own son
Come to help us kinder be
He loves us everyone.

BMB-M 16.12.07

Gloria B-M
Briar House Residential Home for Mental patients

Apart from her poor sad son
A poor frightened furtive creature strange
Since Mum was taken captive
His shirts undies n'er change
Poor Gloria we know not what triggered this mental section
When viewed her bungalow immaculate direction
Hardly the dwelling of a lunatic raving
Rather of a house proud little lady
On polishing cleaning slaving
Was she frightened to open the door to mental social workers
As lone ladies wise persuaded
So they smashed the door when she solitude craving
Was she frail from a tummy upset for of vomit a patch
On her sparkling clean duvet cover with pillow to match
And feeling oh so weak and poorly
Did she dread intrusion
Data protection prevent knowledge sorely
E'en the past history only strangers paid servants of state are told
And ofcourse her sad son
Such is the plight of lone mental patients old
Is it protection of divorcees and HIV
That transparent viewing of circumstance not see
Data protection surely cannot hide
Necessary facts that relatives must find
Or nurses doctors and workers grave crimes may committed

And no caring relatives allowed transparent viewings admitted
Although traveled to care when no paid state servants there
And help was required
Caring relatives but not 'next of kin' label acquired
Poor sad Christopher told everything but 'oer head overflow
But those who could influence her destiny not given to know
E'en the G.P. had the telephone clear
To call caring relatives when they need to be there
But this had not done
Because Data protection had won
However stranger lawyers, 'Power of Attorney' acclaim
Total viewing of total situation attain
Yet caring medical relatives, in-laws
Gloria's welfare wish to guard
From all information rudely barred
Data protection the officials ace card
No we can't tell you where she's been taken
'No, she's not dead' but her good health forsaken
'No don't ask more because we can't tell
If we do 'Data Protection' will give us hell
'Right, how do we know poor Gloria's not died
And you're hiding a nurse or Dr Shipman who's lied
We'll shout to the roof tops to find where she's gone
To police, to the newspapers to investigate con
But be sure we'll not rest 'til we find where she's lay
Our dear brother's widow we'll search every way
Tell us now or pandemonium expect
Let out your secret transparent elect
Dr M will put himself on trial direction
If he refuses to reveal the situation'
At last he reveal her whereabouts
But would not tell the ins and outs

'You'll find her cared for in Briar House about'
Where sad elderly mental patients see their lives out
And full measure pills are doused and thrive
Until they don't know whether they're dead or alive
After five months we now her eventual find
With arms outstretchedexstatic
Our names immediate brought to mind
A walk in the garden
Our goodies munched down
All reunited the smiles of the 'found'
She enquired of each child
How each family fared
Eureka we've found her
Much sadness was spared
Although a three hour trip by car trip round
We visited as often as spared from home ground
But we noticed her voice
Had almost vanished in sound
But our medical thoughts would remain unfound

Dr M was not allowed to discuss
There's 'Data Protection' and all the fuss
So our medical input in the past of import
Was now rudely disgarded and clearly not sought
It was our family input Cushings disease once diagnose
Not found by another's doctor, the symptoms confuse
Never should observant medical eyes be dismiss
For death may be prevented by listening to this
Vast loss of weight, diabetes O.K,
Could it be cancer
No investigations to say
This rudeness so harmful

To patients welfare
How could data protection be justified here
A cake for her Birthday in August and song
A child to bring joy and smiles along
Pressies delight she tried hard to speak
Her head wobbling wildly
Her voice was so weak
As tears from her eyes so sadly leak
The doctors concerned that
Her head in constant rotation
Meant side effects of drug election
Our concerns we mention
To staff but no changes thought fit
6 months from first seen
As Christmas alight
Dressing her room
In trimmings so bright
More weight loss more frail
Hardly responding to hearty and hail
She was sinking fast

She now knew her sweet house
The lawyers had emptied and sold under her nose
She'd never been back to sort
The small treasures in the past she'd bought
Things she and Guy had gazed upon
Things that they loved. things that shone
No good asking Christopher who'd agree
With all bureaucratic suggestions plea
For Power of Attorney he'd not been thought fit
Yet used for the nod for
House clearance and sale sit

We know through the courts the lawyer act
But why sell the house when no bills were unpaid
What a shock before death to have one's things waylaid
Sufficient would be weeding, periodic property in tact
Now it had been sold was a harsh heinous fact
What a liberty the law and the Government take
Before she yet buried such liberty make
<u>Without an essential prior visit in wheelchair take</u>
How powerless and shattering to morale
To shake a woman's home thus foul
She was delivered a photo or two
And to Christopher some things
That the house clearance man would do
No relative consulted or friend
As to which and what her attention lend
From then she sink so fast
And now is not long to last
What had this lady done to suffer such deprivation
Not even to view before decimation
And yet money not required for her hospital stay
So it wasn't sold in order to pay
For if 'sectioned' the state bear the fee
Therefore what a gross liberty
Friends and relatives kept at bay
So only paid servants have their say
Data protection is the blocker for friends
So deprived is kindly help they'd lend
Never mention 'Data protection' to me
It protects doctors nurses institutions
But never Gloria, never she!
I know not
For they'll not tell

Was it that you refused to let them in
Because fear you befell
Or feeling frail and most unwell
They then the door broke down
For your schizophrenic drugs, your privacy sack
Because a court order some 15 years back
When a minor escalator episode was blown high
She said you brushed roughly when passing by
Because of late your pills not willing take
A Hitler lesson they decide to make
They used this event a lesson to teach
Removing you from distraught husband's reach
Of necessity he deteriorate
And to the bottle he did take
And he eventual died of that
His liver cirrhosis terminal sat
Then you were lonely so far away
Where were those friends a kind word say
But you kept your house in immaculate state
A very private person intrusion hate
But now you were invaded they forced your door
Because you'd not taken pills which they implore
They say you'd put yourself at risk
Wrenched you from your bed at dawn
Not even teeth or glasses all forlorn
Because non-compliance with pills
No English gentleness this fulfills
Why did they not your kind doctor relatives ring
The number G.P. given to bring fast on wing
This I can only surmise
But to find it accurate
Would be no surprise

*The facts I must find
For it brings dread and fear
To little lone ladies
When no friends are near
When no-one will tell
Those who care
What sort of appalling state of affairs
Do we have here ?
Never mention 'Data Protection' to me
Nurses Doctors institutions it protects
Never Gloria, never she.*

BMB-M

My Mother Margaret Gwendoline Sarah Barnard (Nee Read)

Born 5.9.08 100 years ago
Daughter of Jonathan &Emma Read
At Providence House Ravensmeer Beccles Suffolk

I think of my mother often and long
God's treasure of selfless love so strong
Devout, with so warm a heart
Gentle, loving, the song of a lark
Organised , independent and vigorous supreme
Never happier than her children upon the scene
Life cruelly with great sadness imbue
Left at 35 with five and one babe due
When cruel pneumonia to death drew her beloved Jack
And from warm family life immediate drawn back
Slave-farming gentleman his dozen men gone to war
Now spirit rose and left his family he did adore
Rumburgh Suffolk wept with grief
Distraught the loss without relief
In his prime mere thirty five years old
In Barnby Churchyard still and cold
The great barn house they must vacate
For a tenant farmer acres rake
And from this cruel, cruel blow
Sudden life took different flow
The day after poor Jack's death
The war took refuge house bereft

All gathered at grandparents idyllic farm
Ancient Wissett Lodge, found sudden alarm
A British Lancaster Bomber's pilot crashed
Shattering precious lead windows smashed
Sudden this ancient treasure serious destruction
No longer held any habitable function
Although struck the day after dear Jack died
Major catastrophe the family stoically defied
Sadness doubly at that Christmas time held
But to another relative's idyllic farmhouse spelled
Feigned merriment and kiddie stockings filled
To cheer the little ones as tears o'erspilled
Whilst everyone's hearts with grief were breaking
This kindly family ne'r Christmas could forsaken
This close family grievous daze
As at Suffolk countryside in tears they gaze

For 5 years widowed Margaret's children split
The five safely to boarding & relatives fit
Poor Margaret from precious brood now scattered
But in her frail state their welfare all that mattered
She was heart broken and baby due
Command did the two wonderful families pursue

Her five warm kindly sisters, all farmer's wives
She stayed at each farm in turn, rebuilding her life
Each nurturing sister Margaret
As dear Reads yearn
Tried to cheer in her grief and depression to turn

She'd had a priviledged and plenteous childhood

Sweet infant born to Emma and Jonathan Read
In all the snowy frills delight the family feed
Eleventh infant to joyous thrill the throng
The house was all agog with family hither and thither
Tiny hands, black curls and porcelain skin
Exquisite creature eyes wide pure within
Brothers and sisters all peering for a peep
Treading so quietly so not disturb her sleep
Mother sweetly happy as her infant gently lay
Mother luxuriously resting essential doctors say
Enjoying her child with bonding sweet
Responding to the slightest cry and squeak

But a year hence
And barely was this child tottering on tiny feet
And another was there born
And delicate little Elsie
Showed her tiny form
But now Margaret's mother's love sorely need
As this weakly sickly babe she fought to feed
Needed all attention to this infant save
Poor little Margaret too young to be brave

Kindly father saw this infant fade and sad
Straight way upon his shoulders sat her smiling glad
Firm friends from that moment
To the end of his ninety years
Sweet Maggy Read black curls abobbing
Laughter replaced as mopped her tears
For her kind Daddy was the greatest fun
For all his children especially this tiny one

In beautiful Beccles to this wonderful family born
Later to their moated farm with waving corn
Where ducklings their mothers in single file follow
And larks sing high, thrushes blackbirds
And swooping swallow
In ancient Potters Farm Dutch gable adorn
Of ancient construction English oaks
Pleasing beams and blazing inglenooks
Secure and beauteous extreme
This very Englishness imbued in beam

But Emma would only move when all
Modern electricity and water install
With less smoke, candles and fires
Which meant three miles of electric wires
From Beccles to Ellough to dig
In order poles and wires to fit
In this priviledged farm of charm
The Reads settled warm and calm
These tinies picked buttercups and daisy
In the meadows green stroked cows so lazy
Nuzzled horses noses soft
Played in hay up in the loft
Playing safe where trees grow tall
Upon parent's land where night owls call
Ducklings scuttle on the moat
Cock a doo the cockerel choke
Chickens friendly peck and scratch
Until safe from foxes close the latch
Inglenooks ablaze the logs alight
Flickering the beams so ancient bright
Warm and gentle family kind

Adored this setting now they find
By the trusted Steward run so well
The horseman, cowman hedger ditcher tell
And the dozen men include their older brothers
Learning the ropes from less educated others
Jackaroing on their father's land
Learning the art from the labouring band
Before each given his own farm
Where ignorance would cause alarm
Must wait 'til lady of his choice secure wed
To tend his tum and make his bed
The dual welfare securely sound
Safely in isolation bound
For that is the farmer's life
For that he needs a kindly wife
With jovial smiles the Reads were close
Cook and washer woman loved them most
Materially and emotionally rich endowed
Aware God's deep love this family proud
And of each other, a closer never seen
As seasons clothed from gold to green
Gradually 5 boys and 7 girls made
Marriage vows and flowers in Church parade
Exquisite pintucks and Victorian silks
With tiny bridesmaids and pages in kilts
The carriages and horses mount the hill
To Ellough Church ther pews to fill
Infant happiness enriching the Reads
Each rejoicing in sibling treats
A family deeply steeped in family affection
Of a warmcaring supportive direction
Amid rural agricultural beauteous land

Tranquility routine strong labourers hand
The rake drill roll will follow plough
As wheat barley oats and beet to sow
Sown meticulously in season
Barely a weed allow
With regularity to milk the cow
Churned for collection over the moat
Jonathan Read most jovial stood
Wrought of the warmest heart you'll ever find
With his beautiful Emma and family kind
Always a cook employed and another at table
Washing taken to Beccles washer woman able
Another caring for the tinies as arrive
Of all 12 children only one babe not thrive
In this perfect environment young Maggie grew
She and her sister lucky to be one of the few
The adored youngest of this fabulous tribe
Who fun and love was all imbibe
Eldest married and running own farms
With their own infants giving joy and alarms
This family was so large and close
That outside friends were few at most

Maggie and Elsie growing up
These two children stretching their limbs
Mid country trees and grazing
Horses galloping and cows lazing
Cuckoos Robins Blackbird Larks
Golden field waving
Then winter stark
Inseparable playmates rarely storm
Idyllic plenty nurture form

Maggy to the Leman School bright
Elsie to another private school
In Beccles alight

The house under Emma's strict supervision ran
Daughters work outside the home she ban
But allowed to run charitable dances at Sotterly village hall
Drawing room singing their lovely voices call
Cards played regularly with family and friends
Amid much light hearted ribaldry lends
Always devoutly at Church for Sunday matins, voices fill
Ponies and traps ascended Ellough Church Hill
A fine laden and hospitable table seating 24
For Sunday lunch usually more than a score
A blissful country Edwardian life
Maggie was too young for First World War strife
Two brothers were feted when they return safe
Maggie was ten when feast for them made
What welcome what fun the brave brothers to greet
After fighting for England so proud was the meet

Maggy's aged 11

Moated farm with cooks to fill the table
In a loving family of 12 children
Tennis court and many horses in the stable

Maggy gets rheumatic fever

Margaret a fun child great swimmer apace
Challenged a friend across the Waveney race
She won the race but was struck down

With rheumatic fever the scourge of the town
So frail for a year
On the school scene not appear
Her poor little joints so painful to move
Struck immobility no medicine to soothe
For she could not walk for a whole year
Gently nursed by her family from dread family fear
Blinking her lids the fever subside
Family jubilation when death she defied
The First World War was over and England rejoiced
So many lost lives, no more hear their voice
But little Maggy her own war against illness had won
Gradually new health strength and recovery begun
At last on the tennis court and at school returned
To be with her friends and school she yearned
Amid beauteous fields and charming moated farm
Summer sunshine and laughter replaced alarm
This family with love and Victorian order Blessed
Were kindly Christians a close family caressed
Joining farming community at Ellough church
All welcoming Margaret from death gently nursed

Pony and trap to Beccles to school

The horseman brought their trap to the door
'Be very careful' their anxious parents implore
As Maggy confident smiling the reins took
Bob her sheep dog hopped off at the gravel pit
And waiting watching stood
As the two little girls of 11 and ten
Drove off smart in their school uniforms then
To the Sir John Leman School for Maggy and Elsie another

Faced driving to school or boarding like mother
From Potters Farm a few miles by Kitty the pony led
Then left at the Black Boy to be groomed and fed
Whilst the little girls at school spend the day
Energetic little Reads at work and play
Then at the trot with Kitty to collect faithful Bob
Waiting all day at the gravel pit knob
To the arms of their loving parents for tea
Through sunshine and storm relief them to see
The only child at her school a pony and trap to drive
To school, truly a heroine her friends contrive
Whilst Elsie, a year younger never reins take
Big sister had all the decisions to make

Christened "Paddy the next best thing"
Maggy was a fun child playing tricks
On her adoring family
Apple pie beds did fix
Her brothers one day
When she was dressed in a beautiful tennis white dress
Threw her in the then muddy moaty mess
'Paddy the next best thing!' they her Christened
Her Mummie was not well pleased!
Emma said 'you should have listened!'

Her mother Emma
She herself always beautifully dressed
With 'fronts' of finest lace
And tailored dresses and lovely face
She had a priceless collection of Dresden China
In a lovely cabinet the children loved to gaze
With fine ladies sculpted in delicate grace

A beautiful woman as were all their daughters
Much sought by the finest of the county
Well protected by their parents aware of precious bounty
Never allowed to mix with farm hands
Only gentleman with ample lands
Emma's only sister died when Emma was away at school
At St Mary's school Bungay a ladies' pool
She visited her sister as a spirit to say
She'd left her body's last breath on that day
At her dormitory window Emma was distraught
Not comprehending the message just taught
For the rest of her life this sister hovered around
Sometimes appearing others not found
All through Emma's long life to the nineties
Her guardian angel delivering God's light ease

Read family tragedy- their firstborn Percy dies

But in 1934 their first born Percy they adore
A telegram arrived to say he'd been seen no more
He'd visited England with Jean his Australian bride
A few years earlier with immense pride
Celebrations great this marriage to fete
But now he was gone – no sound to make
Whilst visiting his distant New South Wales distant
Where house and land managed by steward's hand
At his farm Percy left his car
And travelled with his friend so far
To enjoy a day at a polo event
With his friend conviviality lent
Upon their return car and steward had vanished
Go your way he said to his friend

Situation I'll manage
Sadly later upon his land down a well
As gathering rooks gathered their grim tale to tell
Australia combed from coast to coast
For the villainous murderer sought for most
Using Percy's cheque book, gold watch and car
A bank teller called Police in a Perth bank far
World press revealed this villain found
For 15 years the Australian judge impound
His wife Jean and Percy's family a greatly distressed scene
Too trusting had this lovely man been
His dear wife Jean who all those years back
England's snowflakes delighted had caught
After 15 years of villain's imprisonment
A passage on Mauritania had bought
Fleeing to England, fearful that villain strike more
To sanctuary of the kind Reads she adore
To England on family farms to stay
All loving this charming lady with her lark's voice each day
For several months round the family pianos entertain
With operatic and favourite tunes when stay
Her cousin the last with Caruso to sing
At Metropolitan Opera House in new York rapture to bring
A great treat in London to Bless the Bride
And a great night at a smart hotel sweet Jean provide
For this lovely family's hospitality her generous grace
This sad farewell they'd ne'r see her face.

When Maggie was twenty she meets her love

One day in May when blossom bright the trees filled

At this idyllic farm over the moat acres tilled
Our Margaret was busy wallpapering the hall
When unannounced her father came in
With a dark handsome gentleman tall
Young John Barnard was educated from the finest family with land
He would be perfect for beautiful Margaret's hand.
Instant pairs of eyes engage in romantic charm
Her parents were delighted with this possible balm
No better match for their adored daughter.
She sudden remembered that she looked a terrible sight
How could she impress as such a messy sight
She blushed with shame to be thus caught
But he was enchanted and ne'r take his eyes
From her beauty sought
Invited to dine when she dressed so fine
The maid gave a wink as she served the wine
Always the servants their young men approve
This match from start radiate true love
Their love grew strong and soon marriage bind
At Ellough Church upon the hill happiness find
The ponies gladly sprint the ride
With Margaret in exquisite white inside
A joyous day and smiles abound
Maggy has her farmer found
Never had Barnby such smart cars seen
As clustered round the Holly Farm green

Maggy an adoring mother at Holly Farm Barnby

The villagers delighted that their young squire
Had found a bride they all admire

Soon the babies eventual arrive
A bonny family healthy thrive
A boy Michael first blond and blue
Then a daughter Anne in two years due
Another daughter Barbara children three
Never too many grandchildren the Barnards see
Then little redhead Jean another sweet child
Then Grahame a fifth child mild

Second world war
But Hitler spoiled this family scene
As his black clouds gather o'er this farm so green
The farm was let and family leave
Too close to Lowestoft where bombs do heave

White House Farm Rumburgh
Jack dies

In peaceful Rumburgh on White House Farm
On father's Wissett Estate in Suffolk pasture calm
Blissful setting but Michael at Rumburgh School
Bullied badly
So to Wissett School each day a mile to walk, sadly
No bullying children safe here
A kind little school Miss Jeffrey care
Sundays formality at Wissett Lodge old
Where Suffolk accent from children tease and scold
Smart lunch at Abbey table
Where 12 disciples stand
Best silver by each child land
Behaviour fitting children must learn
Littles Barnards ways must turn

Weekly freedom must be curbed
Or never smart ancestors served
Sweet Maggie wanted her children happy to be
She wanted sweetness not smart harshness
For her little children, her plea.

Tragedy hits poor Maggie's family

Poor Michael at twelve a horse his face kick
Then a few days later his father fell sick
Of tetanus and pneumonia poor sickly Jack died
Leaving great grief for his family five.
With labourer's all at war
Poor Jack had no support
The night of the fever the ambulance came
Three little girls in their nighties shivered at the top of the stairs
For the last glimpse of their father in tears
The next morning
To cut hay for the stock Maggy had to climb the stack
Four months pregnant, she'd never before worked on the farm
She mounted the ladder with fright and alarm
But must feed the cattle to keep them fed and calm
Maggie stayed close to her love and poor little boy forlorn
Both in Ipswich Hospital her heart wrenched and torn
Her dear Jack died with her by his side
Michael a mask wore the ravages to hide
As his mother cuddled her child her bleeding heart break
Rumburgh farm she must forsake

Then staying at Wisset Lodge a sanctuary kind
All sleeping a huge explosion in front of house sound

As a British Lancaster Bomber make crater in ground
All windows smashed in this medieval mansion
The family near followed their poor father and son
A day after he died the beloved house smashed
By the aga warm
The whole family shelter the storm
Singing hymns and songs with sweet Grandma to lead
Next day to Pond Farm Worlingworth
The family of four to feed
Christmas was but four days away
With stockings to fill and children to play.
All their toys and beautiful dollshouse
By their favourite uncle Artie made
Never to be seen again
Oh War and disease how you have slain
These children so close now split 5 ways
To boarding schools and kind relatives in daze
Their lives for ever changed
Poor Maggie ravaged in her soul so deep
Her whole life mangled and her darlings
Separated perforce or dead
And another infant due soon to be fed

All leave White House Farm Rumburgh
And now widowed such cruelty fate elected
Finally sweet baby in May 44 she ope'd her eyes
This fatherless child with lusty cries
Exhausted Maggie her baby in her arms
Suddenly looked up and there was Jack
Her dear husband momentary was back
Smiling at her and the infant child
Her guardian angel so warmly smiled

And was in another moment gone
Her heart sang instantly loves song
He'd been watching so close
The woman he loved the most

Her husband's spirit momentary smiled there
For a moment rejoice this angel of care
He'd been caring for Margaret though body no more
But seeing, hearing joining baby and wife he adore
Margaret was thrilled, she'd endured such stress
Sudden parents and baby Stephanie reunited in love to Bless
In Halesworth hospital Suffolk where baby was born
Suddenly happiness Margaret's life transform
Round the dear loving sisters she stayed with this child
Mostly with Elsie and Ronnie and family four
Mid kindness and happiness her confidence restore
All Godly in farming they worked and prayed
The child grew strong and healthy with lively cousins
She played
Margaret and Stephanie secure and safe
With kind Basey-Fishers much laughter made
Idyllic farm life plenteous all
But soon to school at five the call
What of Jack's own farm
It gave cause for alarm
For those out to gain from Jack Barnard's death
Left widowed Margaret and her children bereft
Their own home Holly farm now to deny
It had been rented whilst
He on his father's estate farmed
To be further from Hitler's bombs
And the destruction alarmed

So now home grown Hitlers
This bereaved family homeless make
As scheming and treachery
Margaret forced sale of valuable farm make
At war all time low price
Schemer's benefit cheap
But hell is their haven
And devil their leap
Poor Jack in the graveyard in Barnby seal
But no body to fight villains
His family farm and house steal
When Stephanie now ready for school
Margaret confident alone could be cool
So she restored now her brood recall
To make home once more
In Beccles befall
Her parents 52 terrace houses own
Fortunate one vacant in time in town
In Providence Place
His first row he'd had built
When barely a man
Twenty one years he gild
Jonathan Read
For the daughter he adored
Nothing too much
For the six children scattered
To house together really mattered
Barely seen each other for 4 years
But soon got along
With mother love tears
With no money to spare
But gentle well-off family members watchful there

Parents close by
For their daughter appear
They'd been thrust from their
Idyllic farm with a moat
By Hitler's war
When Ellough aerodrome bespoke
Their Tudor Farmhouse demolished
Barns and cottages flat
Although aerodrome barely used
In '40 less than scrap
They found a bungalow
In Beccles nearby
Distraught but no choice
When Ministry says 'fly'
Margaret's daughter Barbara
With these great people stay
Had spent more than four years
In living and play as an only child bound
Now strangely back as one of large family found
Margaret at last had lovingly gathered her brood
Now they'd need clothing and bedding and food
In Barnby before the war there were maids for the chores
Widowhood vanished such luxuries for cooking, dishes and floors
She washed and she ironed
And she cooked, polished all shone
Though by the time the children turned to help
She'd have the chore done
They grew and they worked at their books as were schooled
And they laughed and they quarreled and family fooled
Margaret the mother
Superb organizer she
Sweet lone loving parent

Soon from home they would flee
As was done in those days
No training had she
Not allowed train as a nurse
Much too protected
To mix considered a curse
For the men that they'd meet
Would not be of gentleman farmers seat
For the husbands were most carefully selected
To marry these precious Read girls elected
So now when she wished independent to be
She had no career to earn financially
Dear Jack, of rich family, no Will for provision he made
Of Royal Agricultural benevolent fund she'd not take
But Dr MacLaren a corsetiere about to retire he knew
Suggested sufficiently gentille and only suited the few
She was delighted and off she went to a course
How to fit and gain business source
Wealthy farmer's wives she knew by the score
Soon their ample tummies Margaret regimented more
Her sisters were all corseted as never known before
They'd do anything to help Maggy
The sister they adore
She really loved her newfound earn
No longer to father's purse now turn
Soon she was the saleswoman of the year
Mum of six and working widow confident no fear
The children of her were truly proud
This amazing lady and said so loud
As they married
And trained and own families for some
Such a marvelous Christian mother

No greater they come
With love and wisdom
Hard work and care
24/7 always there
And smiling always and beautiful too
She'd a great sense of fun
Her whole nearly 90 years through
Fifteen happy years second husband Bertie given
'Til he also, a little older went to Heaven
Her God and guardian angel
Had always been by her side
Her children adored her and admired
This amazing creature of happiness
Though life had been so tough
Margaret was a great fountain of love
Smiling valiantly through times rough
A great example to all
A mother with angel Jack above.
With love and gratitude I think of my mother
Exceeding courageous gentle kind

BMB-M 4.3.08

Little Ba

In a hurry little miss independence
When your farming Daddy's out
He's at the NFU dinner
When you made your debut shout
Panic set in as can imagine
Little maid caught her dress
On the washer woman's gate
As she fought with the difficult catch
Terrified she'd be too late
It was dark in early February
She called out 'Please come soon'
By the time they'd all assembled
Little Ba was wrapped up like a cocoon
Her Mummie had coped most admirably
With the babe who'd arrived unannounced
The doctor the midwife her Daddy
Felt they'd all been profoundly trounced
I'm definitely not due said Mummie
But little Ba had different ideas
She'd been far too long in the squashed oven
All those noises she wanted view clear
Now she could see their faces
As they peered at the baby so cute
All so embarrassed that they were all too late
But Mummie smiled and Little Ba snoozed and coped just bute

BMB-M

Is there a recipe for Golden Marriages?

They say what is your recipe you Golden Souls
What is it nutures the 50 year marriage moulds
Perhaps recognition of traditional role female and male
Maybe helps the marriage ship set sail
The wife delighting in culinary needs
With a variety of imaginative foods that feed
The husband protecting and provider able
To nurture wife's security and infants cradle
Always loving embrace and smiles of face
Scolds quickly forgotten and restored to Grace
Hardworking loving and attention exclusive
Grows abundant gold flowers in garden effusive
Easy going natures and ever smiles sweet
Offset craggy setbacks that life ever seat
Warm affectionate words of endearment the norm
Helps calm the edge of every storm
And so most kind the touch and tender the kiss
Which sweetly nurtures marriage bliss
We know not truly where the Golden recipe lay
But magically together its a wonderfully Golden Day

B.M.B-M 11.1.08

Golden Wedding Anniversary

Robin&Barbara Bonner-Morgan 11.1.08

Sweet tender loving golden kiss
Seals 50 years of married bliss
Blessed with loving daughters four
Five grandchildren give fun galore
The timespan seems has gone so fast
With colourful events and memories past
Paths first crossed at Barts in 1954
Medical students in the famous hospital we all adore
Eyes all eyes how came we two caught
In the web of love and passion fraught
Academia, rugby, hockey, tennis, cricket
And weekly dances friendly fun
Brought our lives together
And charmingly romantic passion spun
Jiving light and fleet of feet
Spinning, weaving frequent meet
Touching hands with magic feel
Flirting eyes sweet glances steal
Knew so soon we close must be
This love of immense intensity
The sapphire ring slipped on ring finger four
At Kings College Carols in Cambridge, sealed amour
Engagement announced in The Times Christmas Eve '57
But a month later in secret wedded Heaven
Romeo and Juliettish few people knew
Living apart but a great closeness embue

Blessing in Hampstead Church in May fifty nine
On a divine sunny day of happiness fine
Soon we both qualified doctors proud
Fervent to save lives and help endow
Three yearly infant daughters appear
Gracing our lives until four we bear
Whilst aiming our medicine at exams for treating eyes
With some time spent where general practice lies
At last saving sight together with eye surgeon skill
Fifteen years together this wondrous treasury fill
Australian brilliance year-span seven
Then   Guernsey 8 years of Island Heaven
Then to cross the Welsh mountains high
Music ,medicine and elderly 10 years fly
Then back to Suffolks sunnier clime
Retirement years continue sublime
Now these 50 years have passed
This happy span has gone so fast
Wonderful family, tennis, horses, dogs pussies and sailing
Opera, music, dear friends and exciting eye surgery hailing
Past cliffs and crags and fiercest gales
Smiling hand in hand through these we've sailed
How much longer is anyone's guess
It may be much more, it may be less
We hope with God's Blessings ever near
Our spirits embrace for ever dear
Loves sweet hand in hand adore
Our hearts we will to love for ever more

11.1.08 B.M.B-M.

My dearest Darling Beloved
50 Golden Years of happiness

Of terms of endearment
Be not afraid
For this is where marriages
In Heaven are made
Our love is beautiful
Our love is true
Tender as kittens, lambs
And sweet children
Playing in the dew
Fresh as springtime
Bright roses aglow
Garden of friendship
Sky cloudless blue
Four darling daughters
Most kindly their flow
Five grandchildren smiling
As goodly they grow
We'd fade if we parted
Together we're strong
Our hearts harmony close
In God's love stream belong
As one spirit entwined
Breathing as one balm
Dancing golden in the sunset
Forever cherished in each other's arms

✧

Of terms of endearment be not afraid
For it there that marriages in Heaven are made
My dearest darling beloved
Of 50 wonderful years of rock solid reliability
Attending to our every need with total sensitivity
A golden thread and sun that always shines
An amalgamation of compatible minds
In every aspect of life we find common ground
From appreciating nature and art to making music sound
Sharing eye-surgery and healing the blind
To country life, horses, cats and dogs
In which also the Golden Thread of Love we find
In adoring our close loving family and friends
And the Golden Thread of love they bring
Their instrumental music
And everytime they sing
What a tree of treasure
The fifty years have brought
God's Gold Thread of Love abundant
Light in golden shaft now caught
As we walk towards the sunset
Its warming glow of comfort feel
Only God's touch can bring such treasure
With His kindly Spirit gently heal
God Bless the generosity of this occasion
Our sweet family so kindly give
And all you lovely folk attending
May you also in Golden Warmth now live
My dearest darling beloved
Thankyou for all the joy we've known
Bless your dear loving heart
You are my Prince, You wear the Crown

Barbara Bonner-Morgan's tribute to her husband Robin upon the occasion of their Golden Wedding Anniversary 18.5.08

BMB-M

Golden Anniversary Day

As the memories of our Golden Gathering fade
Into the golden light of time

Glimpse the warm moments
Of the celebration fine
The glorious colours in the lady chapel there
Where our family prayers of thanks
Are of God's love so well aware
Past gold balloons lovely smiling guests
Champagne —sip on the sunlit lawns
Where weeping willows mere ripple
In the gentle breeze
And lengthening fronds
Then in colourful stream to fill
The ancient Aldenham school hall
Alive with more gold balloons, smart chefs
With immaculate hats stand tall
Tables laden with delicious food
Soon near hundred happy guests and good
With Golden Wedding discs identify, calm settle
Relaxed and chattering, in delightful mood dining
Delightful company & delicious feast finding
Grace is said angel voices imagine sung
But shyness conspire not to stretch and challenge lung
He the Golden squire does sweetly praise his Golden lady there
And she declares his every courtly virtue as poetry filled the air
Their love for each other so palpable, warm and strong

From first eyes met magnetic, captivated, exquisite belong
Yet if 'twere possible more strong in 50 years
Devotion sweet, loving, deeply warm , and kindly bears

The speeches toast and kindly praise the golden couple there
And rich poetry and song most sweetly fill the air
Then to culminate the span in rich delicious cake
The fifty faithful years each other joyous make
Emblem with R and B their names to weave
Sweet embroidery so sweet concieve
Entwined and circled flowers endue and mist
Each others eyes engage therein a loving kiss
As each year pass more loving close to come
Each other's presence does warm signify the sun
Then glowing wondrous words from golden daughters four
Present a golden cup to parents they adore
And truly they the gift of time sublime
And their sweet infants five
Make truly gold this life so fine
Then these gold cherubs family all
Make song, poetry and music for all to enthral
And if they, the golden couple have a golden wish implore
It would be to repeat this enchanting day once more
And wish all their family and friends all best in life
God's blessings, good health, happiness
All kindly free from strife
This day exstatic so warmly lit by smile and friend
As sweet farewells are said
Exquisite day must end.
A million thanks to family divine
For giving us this amazing time sublime
For 'twill rest for ever in memories sweet treasures
All their amazing generosity planning perfect measures

※※※

Thankyou sweet family

What a wonderful wonderful day
Our Golden Wedding on the 18th of May
Our sweet warmhearted generous
Darling daughters and husbands
And our adorable grandchildren five
Of love which shone like pure gold
Brought forth a great treasure to thrive
To honour your aging parents soon to be old
Your great efforts and exquisite goodness
Even took the clouds to flight
After days of rain and gloom
Brought brilliant sunshine bright
Your kindly spirits warmed the sweet earth
A truly divine family
To pure sacrificial goodness gave birth
Thankyou a million times
We shall cherish this day
For the rest of our lives
Which will be longer we pray
The perfection of your planning
Complicated musterings to sing
All brought this amazing event
With exquisite loves amazing ring
Beautiful venue Aldenham School make
Beautiful family, lovely guests and gorgeous cake
Golden guest discs and very delicious food
Everyone in fun and joyous mood
Triumphal arch, streamers and balloons of gold

And dearest words from our sweet family unfold
Poetry and wondrous family sing
Just amazing everything
We felt so loved so greatly esteemed
By all our treasures in whom the sun beamed
Of this day we'll ever talk and dwell
A day in which our hearts did swell
With love and pride
With each dear family member there beside
Its palpable touch of sweetness
So warmly wreathed in smiles
With sweet loves elastic warmth
Stretching throughout life's miles

DARLING DARLING FAMILY

May God with you closely walk
Your adoring parents will never find words express
Our gratitude for this elegant party's finesse
To mark the golden zenith of our marriage strong
Abuzz with delight of friends and family belong
May God favour you with Blessings Golden dew
May you each and everyone find love that's true.
All Happiness and Health and Love to you we pray
And again a million thanks from us both
For a divinely golden day.

..R &B B-M… 18.5.08

State Stealing Babies

My babies my babies
Whose stolen my babies
For whom I've scrimped and slaved 24/7
My love my life
My own piece of Heaven
No reward except my love their love
My sweet kittens my doves
Food food always food
Washing ironing tired feet stood
Shopping heavy bags to toil
Drying tears when feeling soiled
Up and down from rest at night
Worry worry with child health plight
Dragged from bed so early for school
Brushed hairs shone shoes
Uniform neat and cool
My babies my children
Bureaucratic thieves state sanctioned
Have stolen you for others
Who no babies have actioned
My chips are truly down
Their power have thrown
Cruel Judge Gefferies action
State satisfaction
Has bastiche played a part
In stealing my heart
A couple of men with state hallowed ways
Where hygiene bears not scrutiny or praise

Have command of my babies which worries me sick
But the state's a cruel master
And so full of tricks
I bore these sweet souls for 9 months for my own
How could any one steal my possessions so bold
How come support is not first given to me
Before action to please barren men is the plea
My heart is aflame with fury and grief
My babies my babies come back and relieve
Even my dear parents whose love is profound
Were rejected as helpers 'til my feet have I found
I've been ground to a halt with drugs of despair and strife
And all I need is help to recover my life
Dear God give me strength to fight the cruel state
Who've stolen my darlings
As I face my cruel fate.

B.M.B-M 2009

Beautiful Wonderful England

You truly have my heart
We've travelled far and wide
There is none anywhere compare
With you beside
Money riches never a substitute find
For this wondrous land and people kind
Your people warm and wise and good
In Christianity deep and firmly stood
E'n if pretence makes seen far gone
Beneath the skin a loyal Christian song
Your hedged meadows smooth and green
Where cows unhurried chew the scene
Fine horses past hedges gallop speed
A flowing tail and mane make heed
Domestic pets cats dogs rabbits adore
Important to the English happiness store
The changing cornfields turn from brown
To green then glorious gold
Inspires great artists then farmers reap
And store in granary fold
East Anglian charm these rolling colours best
Interspersed with ancient churches serve
Each charming village tranquil rest
The Penine range so tall
The Lakelands where the eagle call
Devon Cornwall warmer tighter charm
Rage seas exciting round the land more calm
The multitude of ever changing coastline miles

Brought history Roman Viking Europe styles
A language fine of Shakespeare's ilk
Which finely tuned is finest silk
The language of the world become
By I.T. advance its central sun
It is a land to love so fair
For truly do its people care
Expansive fairness for all to seek
Judgements never flail the meek
A handsome race to match the good
And wisdom curtails evils flood
The gardens matchless colour pleases
Around fine mansions scattered ceaseless
Pretty villages towns of grace
Make soon forget those less of face
Cities sprawling still have core
London is one all adore
Cathedrals of magnificence grand
Cambridge Oxford no greater stand
Learning and healing herein hand
Great hospitals the greatest Barts
Nearly 10 centuries of healing arts
Museums amazing architecture grasp the best of time
Carefully catalogued history from our World so fine
Trees magnificent in every county thrill
With height and breadth well spaced with forestry skill
Its matchless beauty and people fair and kind
Where else will you such variety of beauty
And academic quality find
This Wonderful England

BMB-M

Untapped Medical Research

Maybe each doctor has a secret of science
That's been noticed over decades
Of medicial appliance
Like vitamins and minerals
Will Alcheimer's help
But without website revealing
Suffering no benefit of healing
Like restriction of diet
In M.E. rheaumatoid and much more
May vanish the symptons
And normal life restore
Anecdotal observations
A place have to play
In healing of mysteries
In medicine today
So experienced doctors
Look to the loft of you mind
And invaluable help to medicine
Undoubtedly find

B.M.B-M

The Shaws

The amazing talent of the Shaws
With music pouring from their cores
Their father a organist at Hampstead composing
Instilled his 3 sons with music suffusing
Jules Martin and Geoffrey
From the earliest ages
Were turning new notes
Singing complex new pages
Jules and Geoffrey choristers at London St Pauls
Where musical genius undoubtedly
Quite frequently calls
Poor Jules was a victim of World War one
Before his life had bare begun
Martin at Royal College of music most talented year
Under Stanford's influence also Ireland and V Williams bear
Younger Geoffrey to Cambridge study at Gonville and Caius
Then teaching chose delighting all with energy and ease
Geoff's talent was spotted when director at Gresham School
Moved as Inspector for schools music
Where to U.K. schools he introduced Gramaphones cool
The Shaw brothers two stayed close and directed
Their talents to Church music
Which was greatly affected
Organists both at different times at Primrose Hill
With Percy Dearmer and Vaughan Williams music overspill
So great their contribution
The Archbishop them honoured with Doctorates grand
For their efforts to improve the music in our Churches of our land

With the beauty of sound to please humble, lofty congregations
In 'Songs of praise' enjoyed by many generations
They put their heads together
With Vaughan Williams their friend
Expanding English music to enormous extent
The two Wars marred their musical genius full stretch
Even so publications extensively fetch
'The Redeemer' oratorio by Martin so fine
Broadcast by BBC at world war two
End of line
Both as adjudicators much in demand
Always so kind yet right level command
The next generation no music produce
But Geoffreys son Sebastian acting profuse
Shakespearean actor much regaled and adored
Handsome Romeo was about the train to Stratford to board
When a telegram brought news of the theatre in flame
Consternation struck concern how staging to gain
Disaster averted by town Odean Cinema used instead
With a small cardboard cut-out to serenade Juliette's head
41 films, stage TV in which major lead
A long life of acting a joy to feed
But the fifth generation of Shaw genes makes show
In four musical B-M sisters as warm breezes blow
Singers musicians of highest order
Their ancestors pride would much applauded
Their children also these magical genes bestow
As two to St Pauls and Bury Cathedral go
Singing, violins cello saxophone sound delight
Very fitting for the Shaw gene musical might.
As the 6th generation of music takes flight.

BMB-M

The Barnards

From the Hugeonots with spirit independent
In the forest of Dene with life resplendent
But disaster struck when death intervened
Quality of lifestyle immediate screened
12 children who'd had it all
Life halted life most cruelly stalled
Father died a year after employee embezzled
A vast fortune- no way to repay
When death intervened
And grim had its say
Children from fine schools brought to home poor
To poverty's sad label on the door
Some quirk of French inheritance
Family treasured hierlooms taken
By an acquisitive brother-hier
All pity forsaken
They still had the house on Plump Hill in Michledene
Where happier times of affluence seen
They'd suffered a most catastrophic down deflect
Father and fortune both gone disaster expect
But still the good Lord was still there each day
As mother led them to their private chapel pray
Devotion their solace and hard work their recovery
No servants in the house or hired hands more on land
Was their unusually surprising discovery
All of the children were 8 years and more
Some of the 12 were just over the score
A few needed to school until twelve turn

Important to absorb as much as could learn
Older boys to the cattle
To the home older girls
All hands to the mill
'Til recovery unfurls
No money now to rake out the iron
From their now unused Plump Meadow mine
So left to rot forgotten
No multiplying pennies
Maybe future restore
When iron stores not so many
With mother strong
She routined her throng
To keep wolf from the door be bold
Cows milk door to door the children sold
A laundry service smart
The girls found a most satisfying art
Seeming a life from riches to rags
They soon gathered in their workaday bags
They still had each sister mother and brother
And even learned work to love to recover
They remembered their dear father and brother who'd died
When the lift cables broke with the poor boy inside
They now cared for cattle and land
And soon the place thrived family manned
As they milked slaved delivered and cleared
They found they loved what they'd most feared
With no servants in home or on land
They were proud they could cope with only their own hands
Gradual build-up with mother strong the anchor
Soon thriving despair-dispelled work held no rancor
Soon they were happy industrious so busy with work

And smiles returned to this family fortune so hurt
Far from awkward denial of Baptist type roots
Several boys took to the ministry and to Australia they took
One however went there to his fortune behold
George we think must have been lucky struck gold
Grazier and developments in Sydney wide
Hursteville came forth with his fortune beside
Another of this red headed brood
John Methias a different passage take
As footman to Lord Newton make
Her ladyship had a most lovely companion
Who caught the eye of this young man
In this most dazzling situation
She was a Hacon a Haakan we're told
Spoken of as Royal Norwegian blooded fold
So kind and loving of skin so transparent
Also a redhead of beauty apparent
The Newtons these two wished help in romance
Gave them some money to start business chance
So in Lowestoft butchers shop they bought
And soon others in area too they sought
A fortune they made in sausage-making line
Put to good use buying Fishing smacks fine.
Eventual thirty four the fleet
With a partner Jonathan Slater to meet
Twice mayor of Lowestoft and for
Westminster as M.P. Sir Jervais Rintoull he implore
But not for these two
The country they adore
A country estate and home in Oulton Broad
Until World War two with five offsping thrive
What a wonderful fruitful life

A son Jack a farmer academic Greek and Latin too
Two daughters Frobel trained teachers through
A daughter married a farmer from a Suffolk hall
And a younger son Arthur with father had squall
Off to Oxford for clergyman aim
But convert to a Catholic when Henry V111
Medieval history gain
To his father's Huegonot background seen as serious blight
Because forbears had lost lives in the protestant fight
Father most unamused and conflict ensued
For awhile chill wind embued
John Methias died a year after his beloved farming son Jack
Who left six young children
History repeat there for a fact
That's another story yet to be told
As the next generation of Barnards unfold.

BMB-M

The Bonner-Morgans

Great grandfather the Reverand Richard Morgan
In pony and trap faced hills and moorland
Faced drenching rain and hale and snow
His Blessed flock to care and know
Babies cried as Christened at the font
Enrobed in white and frilled the bonnet
Brides and grooms entranced with each other's smiles
As he secured their marriages the families beguiled
Each Sunday conducted at least services three
As the congregation prayed on their knee
Then sadness on sadness funerals conduct
When life ended slowly or hasty abrupt
As tears flow and kindly word he lend
Its always sad to visit the end.
Always hospitality to the reverend father there
Whether in joy or routine or in despair
A Blessing to his faithful flock extend
Such a priviledge to feed God''s flock
In the pretty hills of South Wales stock
His son Richard named too
In Burton on Trent as a chemist trained
Then brought him some lenses and optician became
Then bought he a fine location shop
In Queen Street in Cardiff his final stop
Famed he became as they flocked far and near
When his cousin drew up fine adverts on all station walls
So bright and attractive there calls
No better you'll find

If its convex or concave you have in mind
Don't go squinting when help is at hand
Bonner-Morgan's most definitely your man
Even at Cardiff Arm's Park his fame shouted to umpire remiss
Go see Bonner-Morgan that 'try' you've just missed!
Sadness hit the family in the 1919 'flu
Sweet Jenny his wife was amongst thousands to go
Geoff their youngest was twelve
At school in England so young
And sisters Olwyn and Nancy
Wynn a medical student other son
Devastation hit that family
Never the same
Poor unhappy Richard
To drink did turn
So grieving did his poor heart yearn
Down went his interest in huge success
Without his Jenny
He was a mess
Always had he in theatre music and arts a great support
Very active his patronage and imagination caught
Even help set up the Welsh BBC
And Geoff read the news
And took minor parts
In new plays and views.
Now that his Jenny had gone his interest waned
So sad he drank himself numb
To lessen the pain
This core of energetic vitality
Had allowed himself to crumble
So far from normality
His lovely home in Dinas Powis

Had weeds grown high
And signs of neglect
For his children he tried so hard
To cheerful sound
Wynn was in Malaya
In tropical medicine bound
Rarely back to view the sad neglect
His daughters and Geoff did their best
To no effect
Cruel the whisky when alone imbibed
It dulls the mind and lets good habits slide
Gone his interest in classy cars
He tried never to travel too far
10 years after her he died
But ten years before
His soul lost abide
Olwen and Nancy and Geoff and Doctor Wynn
Wynn in Malaya on rubber plantations
To rid mosquitos
And care for the sick implementation
A hospital he built in Sungi Patana
Could stretch out the arms
To reach coconut and banana
A fine social life in colonial club smart
Plenty of his kind of friends
At home from the start
Had a flying licence
So took to the air
Wonderful views
High in sky clear
Snakes in the garden
Tigers in the jungle

Bull dogs at the entrance to discourage both
Unwelcome visitors never saw sloth
He met Susan his wife
Who with her uncle Arthur stay
Straight way they enchanted
With each others say
Just a matter of time before setting the day.
Which they did
Not without Shaw parental disquiet
They'd lost a son in Africa from disease
And feared for their daughters health and ease
However in Malaya they delightedly wed
With friends to regale them for family instead
And two little boys Geoffrey and Robin they bore overseas
With armours and cooks housemaids
With luxury and ease
Then to England on holiday 1936 time
To return they wisely did decline
For war ensued and Japan over-ran
Malaya and chaos the outcome and span
On Japanese Rail road men died daily by the score
Women and children in ghastly camps of war
They'd not have survived so lucky to stay
Where in spring sunshine they could run in the hay
A Barts doctor friend's practice to share
So Surrey security and house was for them there
A third little boy was born healthy and bonny
Geoffrey Robin and Giles the trio sunny
In Worcester Park their home
Always so welcome for everyone
In1940 at the the beginning of world war two
London was targeted by Nazi cruel

As Luftwafer bombs and chaos reigned
As evil Hitler ruination of Europe gained
These children to their grandparents house sent
From the London area
For their safety bent
Two years to live with Geoffrey and May Shaw
Retired in Courage countryside store
Sudden invasion with tinies galore
Geoffrey Drusilla Robin and Giles
Ride on their bikes
For miles and miles
To a local private school went
Eager with red caps on bicycles spent
Taunted by yobos as red top matchsticks
How they wished a stone they could flick
The beasts!
In the garden each child had a tree
When chaos reigned or a fight
A roar from Grandpa
'Tree' the naughty's plight
A great squash to fit four children and a nannie
Seven to feed for poor old Grannie
For two years this routine squash maintained
Wonderful grandparents patient remained
When Geoff and Robin old enough to board
To Newbury Grammar excited implored
Lots of littlies in a dorm calm
Kindly a school to keep them from harm
Good academic and sports organized
So that they became good at sport
Was no surprise
Robin boarded through for ten years from 8

Many good friends from this good school make
Asthma was a problem for this child
The staff learned to cope patient mild
Later soon made acclaim in the field
A speedy fly half many tries to yield
Cricket rugby tabletennis and snooker
And bird watching
And later the odd game of poker
Were Robin's love at
Newbury Grammar
Nestlings wagtails and yellow hammer
All brothers one time there to board
All say happy with one accord
At weekends they stayed with the Shaws
Their grandparents at Courage
Lovingly opened their doors
Musical influence there had an impact strong
Throughout their lives remain so belong
The two on to Epsom College
Like their Dad
He a keen athlete Victor Ludorum had
But Rob refused Newbury to leave
The cricket team he could not retrieve
And fearing his asthma would return
He was allowed to stay as he yearned
A place at Gonville and Caius at Cambridge fame
But failed physics and rather than wait
He took up at Barts hospital a medical student place
Rather than wait a year he lucky for space
His physics in first year at Barts to make mark
With Nobel prize winner Rotblat no less
Amazing influence for students we guess

Linear Accelerator for Cancer to treat
A genius for these students to meet
Ofcourse in the cricket and rugby teams
Blissful life at this famous place seems
And second year his darling B arrive
To study medicine at Barts to strive
But that's another tale to tell
Search the whisperings and find the detail.

BMB-M

Jeeralang Bush Fires Victoria Australia

Jeeralang sweet Jeeralang play me your tune
Cicadas singing from dusk to noon
Silver your cobwebs as sun does arise
As mocking cuckaburras cacklings
Rise to the skies
Green and wide your sweet soft green pasture
Tall your gum trees grow
Wattles waving pure gold in joyous springtime
By your shallow waving streams sparkling flow
The valley deep rises to Baw Baw mountains grow
Whilst opposite gentle hills part to Tara Valley show
Between open cut dark warming coal
Shallow beneath the land abundant shoal
Over which the droving cattle bolt in echo fear
In times past before the electric power grew there.
Our cattle rescued from butcher's hand quietly safely graze
With horses gallop toss their tails and manes
Our children carefree laugh and play in hay
Every day is bliss of school and play
5 sweet years this paradise to supp
Away from the city's concrete hub bub
Here the bellbird sing
It's penetrating ring
Here koalas gently snooze gum branches high
Part intoxicated on the leaves against the sky
Here snakes scuttle off to hide in grasses deep

Here wallabies graceful speedy leap
Here shudders of quivering earthquakes
Here in our time minor bushfires make
Which generate shiverings of fast flown fear
But here dwelt King parrots exquisite blue wrens so near
The beauty was so vast immense divine
This corner of Australia Victoria God's paradise of Thine
What priviledge to share with sweetest family young
When time in Australia had bare begun
We a dedicated close loving surgical eye team
Restoring sight to blind and hurt through distance far flung scene
Through picturesque Latrobe Valley from Melbourne to Sydney balm
Along Princes Highway through heat gale storms and beauteous calm
Cataracts blindness cross eyed squints fix
Corneal grafts and detached retinas stitch
Gowned hatted masked together surgically mend
So priviledged as husband and wife patients tend
Iritis infections lacerations lenses to sight improve
Dressings after accidents injections pain to soothe
This team hardworked then leisure family love the prize
As they return with grateful sighs to Jeeralang paradise
To swim in pool cool in pastures green
In scent the eucalypt in exquisite scene
Of laughter family fun and smiles
<u>In this same place danger lurks awhile</u>

Bush Fires

Jeeralang Junction
1969 A quiet day
No fire ban
Early winter
Sunny the cuckaburra cackles
The bell bird calls
The grass is nearly green once more
No longer crackles neath the feet
The farmer collects his logs to burn
He tidies the land
No wind
He strikes the match
But a few minutes later
A gust of wind
Blows furious
The smoke The smoke
Suddenly he disappears
His 3 children all disappear
In the smoke
His wife is frantic
All gone in the smoke
She calls and calls
In seconds the flames sped
Hundreds of yards up the hill
Catching the eucalptic oil filled leaves
Burning the grass
Burning fence posts
Then luckily stopped

The smoke clears
They all reappear
The father and the children
Are all safe
☆

Jeeralang
1971 A parrot had escaped
His chain dangling long
Alighting on the electric overhead wire
He shorted the wires with sudden flame and death
Poor parrot
Nearly disaster for the folk around
Within a few seconds the wind rose
The flames caught the eucalypt leaves
Family evacuated with dog
Sped two miles up the hills
Speeding from tree to tree
The wind dropped
The fire spread stopped.

☆

Black Saturday
South Eastern Australia
Gippsland and beyond
200 people died
Godbless their souls
Feb 7th 2009
Horror terror
Gusty windy restless day
Suddenly the sky looked blood red
To the North
The trees were shaking

The grass parched and crackling making
The temperature 46
All humanity covered in beads of perspiration
Suddenly the 60 miles per hour wind
Brought tongues of deadly flame
Heat and embers of a deadly blast furnace
Jumping from tree to tree
As people animals frantic flee
Clawing as an insinuating predator foul
Searching tiny cracks in the eves of houses soul
To climb in devour people photo treasures life's breathing treat
The crashing flame-devoured houses crashing in defeat
Empty dams empty pools empty buckets no water found
All escaped into the raging heaving ground
The beastly tongues of rage chasing cars and people in escape
Like a million angry monkeys in the jungle hate
Like a high speed train approaching sound
Black suffocating smoke and firestorm raging all around
People panicking
People running refuge seek
Wise people hid in underground bunkers
Hid in shallow creeks
Jumped in dams of water
Many they boiled alive
Many the cool water saved
Others
Took wet towels and blankets
Many this way thrive
Drove for their lives
With their families
Some stopped by flames
The wind screamed

As flame made gain
The car screamed the children screamed
The flames roared
The flames soared
At times flames turned away
Long enough to save the lucky day
The pain seared, drive on the brave
Our children our babies our animals
Beat this devil save
No precious belongings saved in this savage rave
No photos passport or licence to drive we save
Turning this way that way to avoid the flames
Until at last a road a clearing came
A friend, a face of hope
Survive this fiery scope
Others died with their house
Others died In their cars
Others running died
Not bear the heats hot scars
The pain the strain
No more to gain
Only God to bear their sad souls up
To His kind presence solace cup
The whole of the Latrobe Valley was alight
Patches in Gippsland flaming branch in flight
The divine Jeeralangs were aflame
For this hell there was no name
For the devil who started it only shame
Houses blackened twisted flattened trees stripped
People despairing no time for blame
Crying Comparing
But such generosity arose

Instant outpouring goodness
A mountain of clothes
Food sustenance for those lost all their people places
Dazed grief tear stained black smoked gaunt sad faces
From Melbourne
A mountain of money came
To rebuild their homes
Though not the same
God spread his loving arms
To try restore their calm
Through kindly acts
As shocked absorb the facts
Mr Rudd Prime Minister
Assures rebuild each brick destroy
With state money and employ
But never will those lives return
Life never the same
As they would yearn
Cruel Black Saturday
In beautiful Jeeralang
How ever did this
Savagery began

Paradise -Saved

But later some good news there came
To offset fiends part in this shame
As winds sent the rage to Jeeralang Junction
Sudden the wind change in opposite direction
The B-M house & Paradise was saved
Just when we thought it met its grave
The places where times past our tinies play
Was mercifully saved upon this dreadful day

Another Paradise -Saved

Twice Barts Hospital was thus saved
In raging fires of London 1666
When all around to ash was burned
And in the World War Two the moment fix
Holborn incendary ball of flames thus turned
All by a chance change of wind to close the gaping grave
Great Barts of England was spared to continue sick to save

B.M.B-M

Sweet child of Heaven

Sweet child of Heaven
So simply come
To warm with love
Our earthly home
The snowflakes gently
Round the rough stable fall
Soft as thy infant breath
In thy hay filled manger stall
What joy mankind to bring
Here lay this child divine
Wide eyed with goodness radiant
God's son born at this time
No comforts lavish at this scene
But love so wondrous strong
Permeates so warmly
As bright angels round Him throng
The animals quite hush their sound
Restraint and wonder e'en abound
Sweet sleep sweet child in rough manger find
Bringing unending gift of love for sad mankind.

B.M.B-M

Sweet Dean

Sweet Dean gone! Can never be
When only yesterday full of life's spree
First Mandy speak and see her love
Next moment gone to his maker God above
Youth full of strength and flood of hope
His precious time on earth cut short of scope
Oh cruel death why take this loving gem
His beloved Mandy and two sweet babes
So need this man of men
So far from home this fine person from his family took
Immediate desolation, his family by him now forsook
The children cry whilst neither know not why
At 4 and 2 too young to understand their father fly
Too young to know his spirit and his body have now part
When his fine capillaries are blocked to work his heart
Sudden fateful sleep for ever then he took
Whilst she was drenched in tears alone despair
He could mere helpless watch her from up above
Whilst wishing he could dry her tears and stroke her hair
He both invisible and immobile no movement make
But see and hear and think and never them forsake
He went as if to pick up and comfort child who frets
But vapour arms can make no movement yet
Frustration angers loving Daddy up high
Uncontrolled spirit when flesh and skeleton die
But floating there he sees hears thinks loves and cares
The vapour same shape and height and looks aware
But no fed body to house and move this vapour shape

No gravitational pull to ground this vapour make
The spirit which loves now, has no voice take
He grieves the space his family sad between
Them and his spirit to them unheard unseen
Oh sadness profound and happiness cut short
So close and yet so far no touch no more
So yearns the heart to precious hand touch there restore
Whilst hovering above, God's angels soothe his grief
Soothing with their love this saddest life so brief
Easing in God's love and peace and light
Whilst keeping kindly love on family's plight
Here is a good soul dear Lord of excellent C.V.
Kindly loving to his sweet children at his knee
A man most fit to have your light and peace
Envelope him within your love which never cease
He too soon ceased his walk along life's length
GodBless the beloved family, soothe cries and give them strength
May kindly family and friends fill the vacuum left
With love and support to this sweet family so bereft

B.M.B-M

Sweet Dean

Love of dear Mandy's life
Depart in Singapore so soon
Cruel cardiac cut-off strife
A fit and healthy man
At 42 a father dear
Of two sweet laughing infants
A happy family there
Swift out of breathing presence
Such grief for Mandy bear
At the height of blissfull happiness
Stripped kindly presence care
Sweet Jesus bear his soul
To your Godly peace and light
And warmly Bless those left behind
To grieve beloved's flight

B.M.B-M

Beef for the boys

Where are the gorgeous men of yesteryear
Ask the daughters of today
None to match our Daddy's here
And sweet marriages delay
Distinguished educated handsome and charming
But real men not middling alarming
Why can this be what is the cause
Is BSE and no beef the source
For a generation of boys since 1990
Beef was taboo to avoid infection
Mums fed chicken as main election
Feminine meat on plates served again
Suited the girls but not the men
It shews a generation later
And a probable causative factor
Beef is from male cattle almost exclusive
Teeming with testosterone elusive
Note the young men on real beef fed
Tall strong and real men bred
To melt the girls and turn the head
Courtship and family minded meet
Soon to wed and children sweet
The world revolves as millions of years
Protective men to allay family fears
No halfway house for national confusion
To create false family full of delusion
So Mums beef up with strength your boys
Give them manliness the girls find joys

Keep the normality God careful created
Man and woman with children feted.
Not only beef to feed young men
But intake consideration at forty again
Aspirin quarter enteric coated for men
So quickly the grave calls the heart
With rich living and stress a part
Therefore to intake his life depends
To thin the blood and make amends
Make our young men strong with beef
Then at peak save with aspirin death to cheat.

BMB-M

The B-M diet that has been found to help get rid of symptoms due to food intolerances

<u>Water water</u>
No alcohol tea coffee or chocolate oughta
<u>Greens greens greens</u>
<u>Brocolli cabbage lettuce cauliflower</u>
Grace these scenes
But never a sprout
Just leave this out
<u>Garlic</u> yes just suffice
And unlimited <u>white rice</u>
And <u>olive oil</u> to sprinkle over
With tiny <u>sea salt</u> to lightly cover
No cakes no milk no flour nor wheat
But <u>oats</u> can usually make replete
No milk or anything from the cow
Nor sugar eggs ever e'en allow
<u>Chicken and white fish</u> both without the skin
No fruit or other veggies take therein
Or return of symptons this will make
If this diet you forsake
No sauces but this simple fare
Is worth trying if disease is there.
Symptons vanish health return
In 4 days if health you yearn.
Test with a naughty day with wrong intake
Symptons return as fast as you forsake
Then another 4 days to find ease

If you stick to the diet if you please
It maybe many years to thus stay
Even those who's crimes incarcerate
This purer diet the violence forsake
Children hyper from E's and colour
May thrive on this diet like no other
Set up cafes with only this food
So folk can eat out avoiding toxic load
Maybe institute in secure institutions
Perhaps food intolerances are more than illusions
It sure helps with M.E.
When listless feelings flee
Also with antibiotic toxicity
Arthritic and muscle pains and depression flee
Developed by trial and error with medical skill
This diet peace and comfort fulfill
There may be many many applications which need research
Maybe even the cancers will wither and lurch
Since World War 2 many ill products have crept
Into our diets for speed and to be kept
So mothers caterers wise listen please
In this fast food world where little ease
Every crumb the mouth imbibe
Will alter what is there inside
Some can tolerate the toxins no symptons adverse
But others stress and rush serious consequence disperse
Therefore be advised if feeling life's strain
To try restoration with a few days retrain
Your body's precious canal defines behaviour odder
So shake off the blues with simpler fodder
Remember just those underlined
Which are marked and clearly defined

BMB-M

Spring

Glorious spring in all wondrous expectancy
Warm bright light beautiful
With daffodils as proof of winter's night
Disappearing fast from sight
As warm golden glowing sentries stand
Smiling delight on all who love this land
Who love life, live in hope, give joy to others
Spring is the light as earth from gloom recovers
Birds dart weave with charm from branch to branch
Chasing each other with ever flirtatious glance
Pairing in expectation of tinies on the wing
Ensure their species multiply this spring
Birdsong in dawn chorus cacophony of sound
Music to our dulled winter ears around
The trees expectant bud in hope of bloom
For them spring can't come too soon
Soon their patient boughs with colour sprinkle spread
As bright warm sun appear from overhead
Sweet grasses press forth delicate green
To cover brown the plough has seen
Aconites snowdrops primroses
Celandines and cowslips golden more to bring
The colour and delight as springs the light and lovely spring
Embrace with love nature and all its beauty strong
This time is best and so quickly gone
Come on apace and then please pause
For Spring regenerate our tired spirits from the shiver source
Please stay in our grasp and slow your pace
When at your height of beauty light and grace

BMB-M

Lovely lady of light-Diana's departure

What dread element
Has silenced
This mother lady of enlightenment and love
This care to the sick
This betterment of society
This twice Reeve of Bungay
This civic light
This mother sun
Others will strive continue where she begun
She safe navigated multiple surgery to heart
Which lesser spirits would have torn apart
But bronchiectasis and cardiac failure break
This breathing miracle's hold on life forsake
Sipping of Christ's goodness
Through wine and bread
She too soon breathed her last upon her bed
Safe in the belief He'd bear her to His paradise
The sanctuary for the kind and wise
Where pain would cease and angels sing
As grieving crowds from Bungay gather
At Holy Trinity her praises ring
Her love palpable
As pink perfumed roses gently rock
Her peaceful casket green
With its precious fill
Her tight blonde curls
No more to brush and till
This joyous loving heart of sentiments kind
In Heaven her true reward will find

For her gentle nursing efficient and sympathetic ear
Her fun and laughter and her endless cheer
Her darlings grieving left behind
Will miss her courageous merriment of most peaceful kind
Michael his sweet family and sister Susan sad
The grieving townsfolk iconic lady mourn
Bungay continue reap where wise Diana's seeds were sown
Her laughter still ringing in the ear
Her twinkle lights the meadow near
Bless her memory keep it long
Her love is palpable her sweetness strong
Her warmth will ever cheer the angels song
As God's Loving Arms receive
Where Diana does belong

BMB-M

11.6.08

Sweet Angel Mayfly

Sweet speck of love why fly so soon
Before dawn has turned to noon
We'd all have warmly welcomed hold
Another sweet child in the fold
Mere twelve weeks within the womb
Then sadness wrought for you have gone
As angels bear your sweet and tiny form
To God's glorious light leaves us all forlorn
Your mother Sarah profound her sadness hold
Instead of child with heart of gold
Her tiny angel back and forth stays for awhile
Until she sees her lovely mother smile
And always loves this kindly beam
Then back to Heaven's peaceful scene

BMB-M

Jesus

Did you know that Jesus loves you
The ball is in your court
No pressure or harassment
Only kind or gentle sought
Forgiveness is his watchword
If your C.V. poor you feel
Simply close your eyes and pray 'forgive'
To feel the hands that heal
His support then enrich your spirit
And open eyes to warm kind love
Just close your eyes and say a prayer
To feel caring from above

BMB-M

Abigail to Mummie Tara

Mummie Mummie in Heaven which is your star
Please look at my lovely Mother's Day card
Which I made for you and put lots of pretty flowers
It took me lots and lots of hours
Why did you die just before I could give
I wanted you to be here for ever to live
But I suppose you can hear and see me at home
I'll need you to whisper to me when I'm alone
Daddy keeps crying and that makes me sad
I'm trying to be brave and smile to be glad
I wish the doctors could have cured your tum
Then you'd have been here when Mothers day come

BMB-M

Lightning Source UK Ltd.
Milton Keynes UK
07 August 2010

158036UK00001B/29/P